KPEGISU

A War Drum of the Ewe

David Locke
featuring
Godwin Agbeli

White Cliffs Media Company
Tempe, AZ

White Cliffs Media Company
2121 S. Mill Ave., Suite 206
Tempe, AZ 85282

Distributed to the book trade by
The Talman Company.

Printed on acid-free paper in the United States of America.

Library of Congress Cataloging in Publication Data

Locke, David, 1949–
Kpegisu: A War Drum of the Ewe / David Locke, featuring Godwin Agbeli
   p. cm.   — (Performance in world music series ; no. 7)
   ISBN 0-941677-38-9 : $39.95 — ISBN 0-941677-39-7 (pbk.) : $19.95
   ISBN 0-941677-36-2 (spiral) : $29.95
   1. Kpegisu. 2. Ewe (African people) —Music—History and criticism.
   3. Folk music—Africa, West—History and criticism. 4. Folk songs,
   Ewe—Africa, West—History and criticism. 5. Dance music—Africa,
   West—History and criticism. I. Title. II. Series
   ML 3760.L6 1992
   781.62'963374—dc20   92-3213
                                    CIP
                                    MN

Contents

Acknowledgments

It is to Godwin Agbeli that I offer principal gratitude. His longstanding dedication to traditional music and to my understanding of it is the rock on which this work rests.

I offer appreciation to my other principal teachers of African music as well: Midawo Gideon Alorwoyie, Abraham Adzinyah, Freeman Donkor, Abubakari Lunna, and Ephat Mujuru.

I would like to take the opportunity to thank the media specialists who helped prepare the audio-visual documents which are available to accompany this book: Huck Bennert and Eric Kilburn of Wellspring Sounds (Newton, MA), and Steven Scrivani of Tufts Educational Media Center.

I have benefitted greatly from interaction with members of the Agbekor Drum and Dance Society and the Tufts University Music Department (especially James Kachulis).

To members of my patient and loving nuclear family, thank you for letting me "just finish this one." It will be ever thus.

David Locke

Foreword

David Locke's splendid study of a little-known Southern Ewe dance, Kpegisu, is rich in analytical detail and deeply suggestive for further study of Ewe song in particular and West African vocal repertories in general.

Working closely with the Ewe musician Godwin Agbeli, Locke patiently analyzes complex rhythmic structure, multivalent tonal procedures, and deeply metaphorical texts. The book focuses on a single performance of Kpegisu from which it draws a fascinating network of musical meanings. This is not a book to be read passively, as if Locke were merely telling about an-Other musical culture. On the contrary, Locke is concerned to problematize the insider-outsider opposition by inviting readers to play—either silently or out loud—with Kpegisu's diverse and enticing materials. In his explicit analytical moves and the author's methodological self-awareness, *Kpegisu: A War Drum of the Ewe* moves us ever closer to the threshold of a general theory of Ewe music.

Dr. Kofi Agawu
Professor of Music, Cornell University

Preface

*T*his book discusses *Kpegisu,* one of the oldest orally transmitted drumming, dancing and singing festivals of the Ewe people of West Africa. Included are analyses of the rhythmic and tonal progressions of the music, complete scores in staff notation and discussion of the metaphorical lyrics of the songs.

Master drummer Godwin Agbeli's knowledge of Ewe culture is the foundation upon which this presentation rests: his drumming and singing is notated in Chapters Two and Three; his research forms the basis of Chapter One; he transcribed, translated, and interpreted the song texts found in Chapter Three. Based on my many years of study with him (since 1972), the analysis in Chapters Four, Five, and Six is strongly influenced by Mr. Agbeli's conception of Ewe music.

In addition, this book is closely aligned with two video tapes and an audio tape also published by White Cliffs Media Company. One video program, *Kpegisu: Video Master Class,* consists of a musical demonstration by Godwin Agbeli, an Ewe performer and teacher. A second video program filmed in Ghana by Mr. Agbeli, *Kpegisu: Video Documentary Performance,* shows sequences of a performance by Ewe villagers in Africa. The audio tape *Kpegisu: Aural Examples,* contains Mr. Agbeli's demonstrations of the drum ensemble music and his presentation of twenty songs, with examples keyed to the book.

I have designed these materials to guide you, the musical "user," into contact with Kpegisu as performed by Africans. The book stands alone as a viable introduction to the music. But the availability of the audio and video tapes further democratizes the discourse: the African "voice" is heard, readers can have their own interpretation, the communication becomes plural and inter-cultural.

The general subject of African music is increasingly familiar to open-minded musicians. Valuable introductions include books by Bebey, Nketia (1974), and Thompson (1974).[1] Ewe musical culture is well known internationally in comparison to the traditions of other African people. The performance of Ewe music and dance is taught by in many educational institutions throughout the world. Perhaps the best known written works are those of A.M. Jones (1959) and John Chernoff. I myself have already published two long works on Ewe music (Locke 1978, 1987) and it has been the subject of several masters theses and doctoral dissertations, many of which are cited in the bibliography (see especially Anyihodo and Fiagbedzi 1977). These materials on Kpegisu, in other words, are part of an ongoing knowledge-sharing effort by many people—Africans and non-Africans.

The goals of this project can be summarized as 1) archival—to document a portion of humankind's heritage; 2) educational—to teach about Kpegisu's cultural and musical meanings; and 3) artistic—to encourage creative engagement with its forceful surfaces, including sensitive appreciation, composition, and re-creation through performance. I presume Kpegisu to be of interest in its own right as exciting beautiful music—a challenge to learn and fulfilling to play.

Like many types of traditional music from throughout the world, Kpegisu has the potential to become a pan-human art. While not underestimating either the distinctiveness of Ewe culture nor the particular history and meaning of Kpegisu, I intentionally move towards what might be termed "universal relevance" in this book. Although our divergent personal and cultural experiences give each of us a distinct musical sensibility, there is no innate difference in teaching Kpegisu to Ewes and non-Ewes. Accordingly, my focus is primarily directed toward theoretical musical elements such as melody and rhythm rather than local ethnographic information. I hope to encourage respectful, thoughtful, spirited involvement with Kpegisu's music and I assume that a wide variety of valid new meanings will follow from this engagement.

In my view, the Ewe people need not be regarded as an exotic presence. Yes, theirs is a formidably sophisticated musical art but insofar as it is a human tradition, it can be learned. In the scores I have tried to truthfully and accurately document the performed music. The analysis strives for sensitivity to the Ewe musical perspective while, at the same time, providing relevant insight to the cultural newcomer. Just as Mr. Agbeli and I have been exchanging views for many years, it is my hope that "we" (you—the viewing, listening, reading musician, him—the culture-bearing teacher, and I—the advanced student) all will enter into meaningful dialogue with the tradition of Kpegisu.

David Locke

Chapter One

Introduction

*T*his chapter includes a brief history of Kpegisu, an overview of the percussion ensemble, songs and dance, and a description of a typical performance of a Kpegisu group from Ghana. I begin with a profile of Godwin Agbeli.

Godwin Agbeli

Godwin Agbeli traces his talent in music to his paternal great-grandfather, *Adedi*, a great drummer whose spirit he has inherited. In his childhood during the 1940's and 1950's he showed aptitude in drumming. When he and his friends imitated the adults' music-making, Mr. Agbeli played the role of lead drummer. Soon he was taking part in the ritual and social drumming in his hometown, *Kofeyia*, near the town of Aflao at the border of Ghana and Togo. His father, *Anthony Agbeli*, although not a master drummer, was a trusted bell player; his mother, *Sahoshie*, is a priestess in the *Yeʋe* religion and a source of Mr. Agbeli's large repertory of traditional songs.

As a young adult Mr. Agbeli enjoyed producing musical dramas. He wrote scripts, composed songs, arranged drumming, designed the costumes, directed the performances, and solicited the support of patrons. In the late 1960's he was selected by the Ghana government for a training course in drama and soon after he joined the National Folkloric Company under the aegis of the Arts Council of Ghana. Mr. Agbeli learned a large multi-ethnic repertory of music and dance as arranged by choreographers such as Robert Ayitee and C.K. Ganyo. Since leaving the Folkloric Company in the early 1970's, Mr. Agbeli has worked as coach and artistic director of a wide variety of groups involved in performance of traditional music, dance, and drama. Currently he directs his own troupe, the Sankofa Dance Theater.

I have known Mr. Agbeli since 1972 when he was a Visiting Lecturer at New York University. He was my primary teacher and research colleague during my doctoral field research in Ghana (1975-1977) and subsequent visits. Since 1987 Mr. Agbeli has taught regularly in the United States under the sponsorship of the Agbekor Drum and Dance Society and Tufts University, where I am a professor of music and dance. I have found him to be a magnificent performer and excellent teacher. An inventive and forceful drummer, he relentlessly but coolly "pushes the time." I especially love his sonorous singing voice and marvelous melodic improvisations. Most important in this context, he is a patient teacher with high standards who can explain his music to non-Africans without compromising its authenticity.

Victoria Pagnaa Wombie, who plays the bell part on the studio video program, is a member of the *Dagbamba* ethnic group of northern Ghana. For many years a leading dancer with the Arts Council of Ghana National Folkloric Company, she and Mr. Agbeli are old friends. Although primarily a dancer and vocalist, Ms. Wombie is familiar with the percussion parts for a large repertoire of dances. During the summer of 1989, Ms. Wombie was in residence at Tufts University and the Agbekor Drum and Dance Society.

I have studied African music since 1969 with several teachers including Abraham Kobina Adzinyah, Freeman Kwadzo Donkor, Midawo Gideon Foli Alorwoyie, and Abubakari Lunna. My academic degree is in ethnomusicology from Wesleyan University; my doctoral dissertation, *The Music of Atsiagbekọ*, was supervised by professors David McAllester and J.H.K. Nketia.

These materials were prepared over the course of several years. The master class with Mr. Agbeli was shot and edited in 1989 at the Tufts Educational Media Center. I transcribed the music and wrote a preliminary draft during the winter months. Mr. Agbeli returned in the summer of 1990 with the video of the Wodome-Akatsi performance. After the program was edited, he and I had long research sessions primarily devoted to the performance video and the meaning of song texts. Toward the end of the summer he recorded the songs and the audio program was prepared. During the fall and winter of 1990–91 I transcribed and analyzed the songs and then rewrote the entire manuscript in light of the enriched data.

Kpegisu

The Ewe people (population approximately 1 million) live in the southeastern Ghana (Volta Region), southern Togo, and southwestern Benin.[1] The Ghanaian Ewes came to their present territory in the 16th century after a long period of migration westward from Nigeria and their culture shares many features with their neighbors (and sometime enemies) such as the Akan, the Fon, and the Yoruba.[2] Northern and southern Ewes are distinguished from each other by geography, language and culture. Kpegisu is from southern Eweland. In comparison to nearby ethnic groups with strong national institutions of centralized authority (the Akans, for example), the southern Ewe are relatively decentralized. Although the chieftaincies of the southern Ewe (Anlọ, Avenor, Some etc.) are joined in the Anlọ confederacy, the primary frameworks for the day-to-day life of most people are the patrilineal extended family, the patrilocal village, and the religious congregation (traditional and/or Christian). Religious specialists, family elders, and chiefs exercise leadership and negotiate power.

The Ewe believe in a Creator and a complex array of divine forces with whom humans interact to solve problems and achieve their aspirations.[3] A human being's body lives and dies, but the soul or spirit exists before and after an individual's life on earth. Since the spirits of the ancestors play a powerful role, funeral rites are exceedingly important. A key social institution for the performance of music and dance is the funeral mutual aid society.[4] Members of these cooperatives pool their resources to pay for each other's funeral expenses. In addition, the group's performance ensures a memorable funeral and proper sendoff for the deceased's spirit.

Performances of composed repertories by formally organized groups *(habobo)* are an important institution in the Ewe way of life. In the Ewe language *(Eʋegbe)* items of repertory are called Drums *(ʋu).*[5] The performance of a Drum integrates the arts of drumming, singing, dancing, poetry, drama, costuming, and sculpture. A Drum is simultaneously aesthetic and utilitarian; not only is it a manifestation of beauty, mastery, and creativity but, at the same time, it also fulfills a social purpose. Drums are performed at life cycle ceremonies, religious rituals, chieftaincy festivals, and recreational events. I think it is fair to suggest that performances serve more general functions: they promote social interaction (cohesive and divisive), teach beliefs and values, and confer identity.[6]

Kpegisu is one of the oldest Drums in the Ewe repertory. Although it is considered a dance of the olden days, Kpegisu is still performed in contemporary Ghana. The Ewes call it a War Drum *(aʋaʋu)* and accord it high prestige because of its association with their forefathers. Its songs give advice from the ancestors, its dance embodies graceful strength, its drumming exudes power. A performance of Kpegisu affirms life and gives respect to the dead.

In comparison with some funeral, social, and religious Drums such as *Agbadza, Kinka,* and *Brekete,* Kpegisu is not widely known or frequently played.[7] It is a more specialized repertory maintained primarily in communities with an unbroken local oral tradition. Most performers are the kin and neighbors of knowledgeable elders who form the nucleus of the group. For example, members of a Kpegisu group from the village of *Amelɔmekɔfe* interviewed by Mr. Agbeli in 1989 said they formed their group around an elderly husband and wife. These elders had seen the great-grandfathers do Kpegisu and did not want to let it die. They wanted the youth to learn the good sense conveyed in the song lyrics. As Mr. Agbeli put it, "How to sing and advise the children of doing good things—that is why they created their Kpegisu group."

In Mr. Agbeli's opinion, the group from the village of Wodome-Akatsi is one of the strongest exponents of Kpegisu in Ghana today. Their association has many members and seems to perform regularly. Elders of the group tell the following account of the origin of Kpegisu. The paraphrased version draws upon the speech made by the village chief, Togbui Sakpaku, and other conversations recounted to me by Mr. Agbeli.

> *Long ago in the times of the great-great-grandfathers there was a man named Dogbetǫ. It happened that Dogbetǫ's brother, Sowu, went hunting and became lost in the bush, perhaps charmed by dwarfs or the sea goddess, Mamiwater. Dogbetǫ and friends searched for him in vain, but at long last Sowu returned. He sang what became the first Kpegisu song, "I called out, but no one heard me." [See "Agbemewo Me Si O," Song 11, Chapter 3.] Soon composers and drummers created a full type of music and dance based on Sowu's experience. Dogbetǫ himself composed many of the first songs and the people's leader, Togbui Sakpaku, took it as his war drum. Over the years other songs which contain proverbs that teach important lessons for right living were added as the Drum gained more widespread acceptance. Kpegisu was used to send the men off to war, and welcome them home again. It was a dance for men to show their strength, a dance of seriousness.*

In modern times performances of War Drums are discouraged by the authorities because fights often break out among older men who become charged up by their aggressive spirit. Consequently, performances of Kpegisu are infrequent. Major festivals and funerals for group members are the primary occasions for performance. Kpegisu groups usually perform at the *Hogbetsotso* Festival, the annual commemoration of the Ewe's 16th century exodus from Nǫtsie in Togo. This festival is held in Anlǫga, capital of the Anlǫ traditional area, which boasts one of the best and most knowledgeable Kpegisu groups. Kpegisu also is revived by professional dance companies and what are known in Ghana as "cultural groups," that is, theater-style groups sponsored by schools and churches.

Performance

In this section I will outline the sequence of events within a typical performance (see Chart 1.1).[8] Performances usually occur in the afternoon from approximately 3:00 to 6:00 pm. If the performance is taking place in another village or on the occasion of a group member's death, the group may begin with a procession *(Vulolo)*. If the performance is on the first memorial of a deceased member, the procession visits the person's favorite spots in the village. People make believe to be looking for the deceased as if he or she is missing. Everyone knows the person has died, but this fiction enables the group to relive and formally acknowledge their loss.

The performance area *(tome)* is outdoors, often near a shade tree. Group members sing and clap hands from the benches arranged around its perimeter. Drummers *(vufolawo)* sit along one side. Males tend to congregate near the drummers who are all males. Elders, group officials, and invited dignitaries *(amegawo;* big men) sit behind the drummers just outside the perimeter of the dance circle. Women also tend to sit together with female elders sitting in a second row of seats outside the main line of benches.

The performance has clearly defined sections. Executive officers in the performance group usually advise the lead singer and lead drummer on the duration of these sections. After the procession, the slow drumming *(Vu Blewu)* begins with *Adzo,* a preliminary period of dance and singing to the music of the lead drum, accompanied by bells, clapping, rattles, and the high-pitched *kagan* drum. When everything is ready, the lead drummer *(vunoga;* big mother of the drum) plays a special phrase *(vutsotso;* taking/starting the drum) which signals the other drummers to begin. After approximately twenty minutes, song leader cues the lead drummer to end the slow music and then he brings in the fast drumming *(Vutsotsoe)* by raising a fast-paced song. The fast section continues for about twenty minutes until the members' enthusiasm begins to wane. At this point the members may signal their hosts to provide liquor by playing the fast music in short sections (also known as Adzo).

The midpoint of the performance is *Hatsiatsia,* an interlude of singing. The song leaders stand in the center of the circle and the group slowly dances around them, singing. Members are served with shots of gin during the interlude. This section ends with songs in free rhythm that convey a mood of prayer and ceremony, *(Ayodede,* giving praise). The members crouch down in a tight circle for, as Mr. Agbeli says, "When you give praise, you put the other person high and make yourself low." The full drumming and dancing then begins again in earnest.

If it is a group's inaugural performance or if simply if they decide to do so, *Gbedzitsotso* (Coming-from-the-bush) may be added to the normal Kpegisu performance. Typically, a newly formed drumming and dancing group rehearses for several months in a secluded spot. When it is ready to be "outdoored" the members gather at their training ground to pour a libation, asking for the ancestors' blessing and telling them that they are taking the Drum out. A special procession to the village follows. For a War Drum like Kpegisu the dancers' movements bespeak themes of fighting (slashing arm and hand movements) and mourning (hands on head or folded on chest). Dancers adorn themselves with leaves which represent the bush and signify death.

Towards the end of the afternoon the performance is halted for announcements or speeches *(Gbefadede, Nyanudede)* pertinent to the performance occasion. For example, in the Wodome video the local chief speaks about the history of Kpegisu and formally introduces Mr. Agbeli and other guests to the group. In this case, the speech is followed with another praise song. The full music and dance then resumes until sundown. Sections of the performance are listed in Chart 1.1 below.

The Percussion Ensemble

The Ewe percussion ensemble consists of bells, clapping, rattles, and an ensemble of drums.[9] Because each local group strives to be distinctive the exact instrumentation for Kpegisu can vary slightly, but the musical function of each category of instrument is well defined. The bells *(gakokoe*

Before the Full Performance
Vulolo: procession at slow pace
Adzo: slow pace with only lead drum and percussion
The Full Music and Dance
Vu Blewu: slow pace; full drum ensemble
Vutsotsoe: fast pace
Adzo: short sections at fast pace
Break in the Strong Music and Dance
Hatsiatsia: songs interlude, slow pace
Ayodede: giving praise, songs in free rhythm
Return to Full Action
Vu Blewu and/or Vutsotsoe: slow and/or fast pace
Special Display
Gbedzitsotso: warrior dramatic re-enactment
Return to Full Action
Vu Blewu and/or Vutsotsoe: slow and/or fast pace
Talk
Gbefadede: speeches
Nyanudede: announcements
Return to Full Action
Vu Blewu and/or Vutsotsoe: slow and/or fast pace

Chart 1.1 *Sections of a performance of Kpegisu.*

and/or *toke*) play a recurring phrase that establishes the fundamental design of musical time. Other bells and handclapping (*akpefofo* or *asikpefofo*) set up counter ostinati. The rattle (*axatse*) reinforces and enriches the bell's phrase. The highest-pitched drum (*kagan* or *adzida*) sounds a compelling offbeat rhythm. As demonstrated by Mr. Agbeli, the kagan player has a limited but quite effective range for variation; much less kagan improvisation is found in the Wodome video. The medium-pitched drums set up a repeating phrase that functions in counterpoint to the lead drum. In his demonstration Mr. Agbeli uses only one such drum (*kidi* or *kpetsi*); the Wodome group doubles the kidi with a lower-pitched drum (*sogo*). In contrast, when I saw Kpegisu in the village of *Anlo-Afiadenyigba* in 1977 the sogo played many variations using one hand-one stick technique and functioned almost like a second lead drum.

The lead drum (*kpetsitsu*) is responsible for improvising on traditional themes, spurring on the dancers, and maintaining the excitement of the performance. The kpetsitsu is associated with chieftaincy. During ceremonies of state a drummer slings it over his shoulder and plays praise names, special mottoes, and heraldic phrases. According to Mr. Agbeli, at the time Togbui Sakpaku took Kpegisu as his War Drum, a drum adorned with human skulls was used for these functions (*ametavu*; human head drum). When Kpegisu became more widely performed outside contexts of chieftancy, the lead drum became known as *"kpetsi atsu."* "Atsu" is a nickname given to an older male twin, so the name means, "big brother of the middle-sized drum." Eventually the name "kpetsi atsu" evolved to "kpegisu," and this became the name of the whole music/dance type.

The Songs

Like most Ewe dance drumming songs, Kpegisu songs are responsorial. The chorus has three distinct performance roles: *heno,* the song leader; *hatsovi,* the assistant song leader; and *hamemegawo,* the singing group. The song leader selects and begins the songs; the assistant song leaders join him on the lead part; at the end of the leader part the group enters with its own phrases; after several sections of call-and-response leader and group sing a final section together. In my notation the parts are marked L for Leader (heno), G for Group (hamemegawo), and A for All (heno and hamemegawo together). As the video program of the Wodome Kpegisu group attests, Ewes enjoy the multi-part texture created by improvising variations on the modal melodies. Ewe singing entails a carefully arranged contrast between the mono- and polyphonic textures of the lead and group parts. One song is repeated approximately four or five times before the next one is raised.

Although there is no prohibition against new compositions, most Kpegisu songs are old. Many song texts are considered "deep," that is, laden with proverbs whose meanings are not self-evident and require interpretation. Accordingly, Mr. Agbeli's interpretations of the translated texts in Chapter Three are invaluable for cultural outsiders. Songs from other Ewe Drums such as *Afa*[10] (a religious system for divination) or Social Drums like *Atsia* and *Kete*[11] may be sung, especially in the fast-paced sections of the performance. Mr. Agbeli asserts that the true Kpegisu songs are found primarily in the *Vu Blewu* (slow-paced) and *Ayodede* (praises) sections.

The Dance

Ewe social and funeral Drums have a distinctive dance "step."[12] Known as *dzimexe* (dance of the back) because of the contraction-expansion of the upper torso region, this movement seems intimately linked to Ewe ethnic identity. The torso movement of the Kpegisu dance *(Kpegisuxe)* closely resembles this Ewe signature movement, but its lower leg gestures *(ado dede*, hole digging) and arm movements are special. Although it is distinctive, the dance for Kpegisu does not require the extensive training needed for dances which feature complex figures like *Adzogbo*.[13]

As the spirit moves them people rise to dance in pairs or small groups. After a brief waiting step *(afotsotso,* foot taking), they begin the characteristic snapping of the upper back and gradually cross the dance plaza, ending with a cadence movement. They turn around, resume the waiting step, and then dance back. Many people dance at the same time; the dance circle is virtually always busy with activity. Not everyone uses the special Kpegisu "step" and many dancers prefer dzimexe, the more typical Ewe dance. Dancing is continuous throughout the performance.

A Performance of Kpegisu by the Wodome-Akatsi Habobo

The foregoing remarks provide a normative, generalized description of Kpegisu. At this point, I provide an account of a particular event, the December 16, 1989 performance by the Kpegisu group from Wodome-Akatsi. This performance is also available on a documentary video filmed by Mr. Agbeli.[14] The performance had twelve sections.

The Village

Wodome is a very typical, rather small village of approximately 2000 people. Akatsi, the major town of the area, is on the main coastal road from Ghana's capital, Accra.[15]

I: Procession (Vulolo)

The group gathers on the road from Akatsi and makes its way with music and dance to the village dance plaza. The formation is informal in comparison to the lines of dancers in the Gbedzitsotso ritual. Women and elders are toward the front; adults males and females in the center; drummers and children in the rear. The group is lead by an elderly woman who probably has the title of *hadada*, group mother. She carries a straw bag *(kevi)* in a calabash bowl *(kpaku)* containing items such as a lantern the group would need if they were to be making a procession to a nearby community for a wake-keeping performance. (For a song text with a metaphor about lanterns see *Kaḍigbe Tsihe*, Song 6.)

Male elders wear knitted caps, neckless shirts, shorts and large cloth. Adult males wear a shirt, shorts, and a smaller piece of cloth wrapped around their waists; some wear traditional dancing shorts *(tsaka* or *tsanka)* and many young men in the Wodome group have a T-shirt from the local Catholic church. Female elders wear two loosely draped cloths. Married adult women wear two cloths and headkerchiefs; a third cloth tied with a scarf is optional during performance. Important adult women may wear a loosely draped third cloth. Unmarried females wear one cloth and no headkerchief. Many women beautify themselves with padding under their wrap *(gbitutu;* buttocks building). Jewelry is a personal choice of both sexes.

The song leader carries a cowtail whisk *(enyishi)* as an emblem of his special role. In the olden days, herbs might be placed within the handle of the whisk to ward off malicious magic or to charm the audience into loving the singer. The Ewe believe that all things made by the Creator have a part to play in human life.[16] Although most people are unaware of their properties, knowledgeable herbalists can harness the divine power within plants for human use.

II: Slow Drumming (Vu Blewu)

The group enters the dance area. Sitting on seats just outside the benches are guests from a neighboring community. If this performance were on the occasion of a funeral memorial in a nearby village, these seats would be for the family of the deceased. The men and women go to their appropriate areas and begin the slow-paced performance. A table covered with a white cloth is for the group's executive committee; if this were a funeral performance the treasurer would receive voluntary donations here. In this instance, several representatives in the local government sit here with Mr. Agbeli's friend, Emanuel Mensah Xonyo, who brought the group to his attention.

The dancing and singing begins in earnest, but the sogo and kidi have not entered. The group's chairman *(zimenola)* energetically invites two women to dance, raising his hand to call on the lead drummer to play well for him. Later several other men repeat this gesture when they first rise to dance.

The visiting chief wears a cap adorned with insignia of his office. Several men sing with conviction, expressing through gesture the meaning of the songs. These experienced ones keep close eye on the group and insure the continuity of tradition. Women watching in the background from the shade of a nearby house are free to join the performance, but have chosen to refrain. Perhaps they are just visiting Wodome and are unfamiliar with the songs. They probably are not in the extended kinship network with other group members, for as Mr. Agbeli suggests, "Everyone in this group calls the same man great-great-grandfather."

All group members participate in clapping hands, singing, and dancing. Children are accepted and learn music and dance by partaking in the real performance, not through special instruction. A blind man plays a bell with the other instrumentalists. The "group mother" dances from her seat. Although an elder, she is healthy and has a strong feeling for music, dance, and the Kpegisu heritage. We see that this art enables everyone—young and old, disabled and physically gifted—to join together in performance.[17]

Although Ewes regard the bell part as the central guide for musical timing, the double bell is scarcely in evidence and hand clapping and rattles are much more prominent. Good musicians hear the gakokoe phrase in their heads and, furthermore, the rattle part is considered a virtual twin of the bell. Although it is not a rigorously enforced rule, female should clap with hands crossed, men with palms parallel.

III: Fast Drumming (*Vutsǫtsǫe*)

The group mother rises and dances as she walks with her head load. The group members salute her with ululation. Soon, the lead singer cues the lead drummer to brings the slow section to its conclusion with an ending signal. In the brief interval between the slow and the fast music, the lead singer calls, "Aho dze," and the group responds, "Aho ya." This formalized call and response is taken from work situations which require a coordinated group effort. Mr. Agbeli explains, for example, that when fishermen push their heavy canoes into the surf, after one man cries, "Aho dze," the group pulls on "Aho" and finishes on "ya." The teamwork between song leader and assistant song leader is seen when the fast section gets going: first, the song leader lines out a song in free rhythm; when he moves into strict meter, the assistant song leader takes over and brings in the whole group.

A seated woman throws a white towel onto the shoulders of an excellent elder female dancer. This serves as a mark of respect. In a later shot we see the same custom done for the visiting chief. The fast section ends on cue from the lead singer.

IV: Brief Sections (Adzo)

The performance has been going on for more than thirty minutes and the members are getting thirsty and a bit bored. They begin playing the fast music in brief sections separated by short pauses, both to vary the performance routine and send a message to their executive committee to supply them with drink. They even sing a song which means, "The performance is becoming dull. We need drink" (see *Miatɔ Bebeviawo*, Song 18).

Section V: Songs Interlude (Hatsiatsia)

The members form a large circle and the lead drummer goes around offering tots of gin. The song leaders position themselves in the center. Mr. Agbeli reports that the song interlude is their favorite part of performance because everyone will hear them and know, "Yes, this man really is a composer." When he raises a new song the song leader first sings it through by himself and then the assistant song leader offers it to the group. The group dances slowly counter-clockwise while expressing the meaning of the song in dramatic gestures. Towards the end of the song interlude the song leader shakes his head and smiles at someone: one of the group elders is signalling him to bring the section to conclusion and soon the song leader breaks off this section with the "Aho dze" call. The lead drummer plays drum mottos in free rhythm. Mr. Agbeli is not certain if the drummer actually knows the meaning of what he is playing or merely is repeating "by heart" what he has heard his elders doing.[18] One phrase sounds like a piece of drum language taught to me by Midawo Alorwoyie: "*So gbe de ge,*" or "Thunder will boom," an allusive way of saying, "On the day of the fighting."

VI: Giving Praises (Ayodede)

The group makes the circle smaller and the members humble themselves by bending down to honor the brothers who originated the Wodome Kpegisu, Dɔgbetɔ and Sowu. They move their arms in a circle, depicting a proverb in the song (see *Agbemewo Me Si O*, Song 11).

> Leader: *I shouted [but] the living did not hear me.*
> *And they said people get lost.*
> Group: *The stirring stick dissolves in the drink.*
> *Dɔgbetɔ did not hear it.*

Sogbo said, "The stirring stick dissolves in the drink."
Leader: *Dogbeto sent a person to Sowu.*
Group: *He should come, he should come*
If there is something for us to do in life, we do it.

The proverb about the stirring stick means that Sowu, a hunter, has been "swallowed up" by the forest.

VII: Fast Drumming (Vutsotsoe)

The group pauses to get ready and then the fast drumming begins again on cue from the lead singer. The visiting chief dances with the cloth spread over his shoulders as a mark of respect. For me, this custom symbolizes power relationships between leaders and those they govern: the people give their elders respect, but constrain their authority. Mr. Agbeli comments that he does not like it when people put cloth on him because it interferes with his dance movements. "It is good to be simple," he says.

VIII: Slow Drumming (Vu Blewu)

The group changes again to the slow-paced performance. There is no rule to the sequence of fast and slow sections once the performance has reached this stage. Decisions are made spontaneously according to how the particular event is proceeding.

IX: Coming-from-the-bush (Gbedzitsotso)

In this special section which is not always performed, a small number of the whole group forms into lines with one man as their leader; the martial atmosphere contrasts with the informal collective of the opening procession.[19] Women praise the dancers by fanning them with towels, and ululating. The women's call, "Wo va do," meaning, "They are home," clearly indicates that the dancers are depicting warriors returning from the battlefield. Some dancers seem withdrawn into deep contemplation, putting hands on their heads or folding them on their chests as signs of mourning. Others mime fighting with slashing hand movements and quick deep crouches. From time to time the mourners break into the Kpegisu dance, signifying, "Yes, some us have died, but we will carry on with courage and strength." The dancers adorn themselves with leafy branches quickly gathered from near the performance area to show that they are "from the bush." They progess around and through the dance area and then slowly move "offstage."

X: Speech (Nyanudede)

XI: Giving Praises (Ayodede)

This point in the performance, about three quarters through, traditionally is reserved for announcements and speeches. The group's executive committee may give announcements to the general membership pertinent to the occasion for the performance, local news that affects the group, and so forth. In this case, the chief of Wodome, Togbui Sakpaku, gives a brief account of the origin of Kpegisu and then introduces Mr. Agbeli. He is flanked by elders in the group and the community. As he concludes his remarks he asks the song leader for another praise song.

XII: Slow Drumming (Vu Blewu)

As the group begins, a female elder gracefully dances alone across the dance ring. This style is called *abebu*, or proverbs dance. Each gesture has meaning:

Fists on top of each other:	Hold it firm.
Flattened, inward-facing palms:	It is for all of us.
Arms held high:	Hold it firmly and with pride.
Stylish dancing:	Bluff on it.

Mr. Agbeli explains that the woman is commenting on Kpegisu: "Kpegisu is for all of us. It is a tradition of our ancestors. We should hold it firm and keep it well. We should uphold it, and bluff on it."

By this point in the afternoon, the group is losing enthusiasm. It is not that they are physically tired, but that drink is running out. An Ewe expression puts it, *"Aha ko mo nawo,"* or "The drink has finished from their face." It is the job of the elders sitting outside the circle to watch the group's intensity and order more liquor when their ardor wanes.

Ending

Togbui Sakpaku and the assemblyman walk hand-in-hand away from the dance area and part with a stylish handshake known as *asinana* (hand giving). Mr. Agbeli says that the shake has meaning: the men grab thumbs to symbolize strength, join palms to signify love, and end with a finger snap whose sound means, "We are alive!"[20]

∗   ∗   ∗

Mr. Agbeli praises the style of this particular performance. He admires the group's zeal, as well as their lack of rushing (see *Gidigidi Me Wo Kpo O*, Song 15). Indeed, this balance of intensity and dignity characterizes all Ewe Drums. Their performance style aspires to a hard-driving coolness.[21]

Chapter Two

Music of the
Percussion Ensemble

T his chapter contains scores in staff notation of Mr. Agbeli's Kpegisu drumming. Transcriptions are placed before analysis to give pride of place to performed music—the actual stuff, the real thing—rather than critical theory. [1]

In his demonstrations Mr. Agbeli moves systematically through the percussion ensemble parts. First, the instruments which establish the basic feeling of musical time are taught: Example 2.2) gakokoe; Example 2.3) gakokoe and axatse; and Example 2.4) gakokoe, axatse, and kagan. Then kidi, the drum in the mid-pitch range that "talks" to the lead drum, is presented: Example 2.5) gakokoe, axatse, and kidi; Example 2.6) kidi with axatse marking the beat; and Example 2.7) gakokoe, kagan, and kidi.

The lead drum is demonstrated in three settings: Example 2.8) gakokoe, axatse, and lead drum; Example 2.9) gakokoe, kagan, and lead drum; and Example 2.10) gakokoe, kidi, and lead drum. Example 2.11 adds Mr. Agbeli "playing the drum with his mouth," that is, reciting drum syllables for the lead drum part. The many versions of the lead drum part enable us to get a good understanding of Mr. Agbeli's lead drum style.

In comparison to the Wodome group's use of contrasting slow- and fast-paced sections (dotted-quarter = 118 and 156), Mr. Agbeli presents the drumming in only one, moderately fast tempo (dotted-quarter = 130). Further, he shows only one kidi phrase, whereas the Wodome group has a different kidi-lead drum duet for each tempo. Although these differences will be discussed in Chapters Four and Six, the emphasis in these written materials is on Mr. Agbeli's demonstrations.

Readers are urged to forge a direct link with Mr. Agbeli's music-making before considering staff notation and musical analysis. Most likely, a reciprocal study of audio-visual programs, score and analysis will be needed before most readers can "hear" this complex and unfamiliar music.

Musical Notation

Many systems for the notation of African music have been tried.[2] I choose to work with staff notation because it is a widely known, powerful means for the graphic representation of music. Although on first impression it might seem that staff notation would grossly distort the African musical conception, this has not been my experience.[3] The logic of Ewe music lends itself quite well to staff notation. As is true for all music, however, notation never conveys the full musical reality but only provides a surface picture, a means for patient study. This is precisely why audio and video programs are available to supplement these materials.

The analysis in Part Three delves deeply into musical nuance but these transcriptions strive for clarity.[4] The primary objective in the scores is to indicate timing and polyrhythmic interaction as clearly as possible. All parts, therefore, are written in 12/8 meter and beams are drawn without exception to the dotted-quarter beats.[5] Polymeter, in other words, is not "up front" in the transcriptions but must be inferred by perceptive readers. Rhythmic multideterminacy in Kpegisu's drum music is discussed at length in my musical analysis.

Rests do not represent silence or a stoppage of sound but are used to mark onbeats on which strokes are not initiated. Although tones played just before onbeats do, in fact, prolong through the written rest, ties are not used in the drumming notation; readers are asked to accept this convention because it most clearly shows when tones are struck in relation to the all-important four-feel meter. Measure numbers indicate the sequence of notated measures and are not affected by repeats. In the lead drum demonstrations, the gakokoe, axatse, kagan, and/or kidi parts only are written for several measures; the written indication "et cetera" means that a phrase repeats exactly for the duration of the example.

In my system of notation the sound quality (stroke type) of a tone and the hand (strong or weak) with which it is played is indicated by the location of note heads on the staff, as demonstrated in Example 2.1.

The gakokoe is struck with a wooden stick on either its lower- or higher-pitched bell. The axatse is struck either downward against the thigh or upward against the palm. Every drummer uses two wooden sticks. Kagan

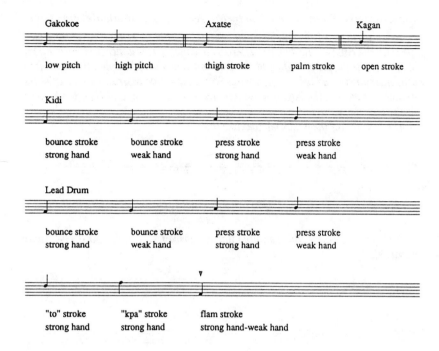

Example 2.1 *Key to notation of drum strokes.*

strokes are always "open" tones and its pairs of tones always are played strong hand first, weak hand second. Kidi plays either bounced open tones or pressed closed tones ("dead" strokes) with both hands. The lead drum also plays bounce and press strokes with both hands, plus two additional strokes with the strong hand: "to," the drum skin is muted with the weak hand stick and then a bounce is played; and "kpa," the wooden side or rim of the drum is struck. In the transcriptions only "kpa" strokes have stems down. ("To" and "kpa" are mnemonic syllables used when a musician "beats the drum with his mouth;" for more information see Chapter 5 and Example 2.11 for data on drum stroke syllables.) A flam-type ornament—two bounce strokes played in rapid succession, strong hand then weak hand—occasionally is used.

Transcriptions (From instruction by Mr. Agbeli, also available on video.)

Today we are on Kpegisu. *Kpegisu is one of the oldest drumming of the Ewes, especially the Anlos. This dance is a very slow dance, a war dance performed by the old folks of the people of Anlo and the Ewe in particular. They play this with four main instruments added by the rattle. So we have five instruments in this: the gakokoe, the axatse, the kagan or adzida, the kidi or kpetsi, and then the kroboto which is the master drum.*

The rhythm [of the gakokoe] goes like this.

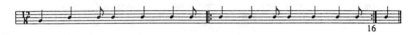

Example 2.2 *Gakokoe.*

And then the axatse added another flavor this way. Now let's hear the bell [with the rattle].

Example 2.3 *Gakokoe and axatse.*

And we have the third instrument, the kagan. Now let's hear the combination of the bell, the rattle or the axatse, and kagan.

Example 2.4 *Gakakoe, axatse, and kagan.*

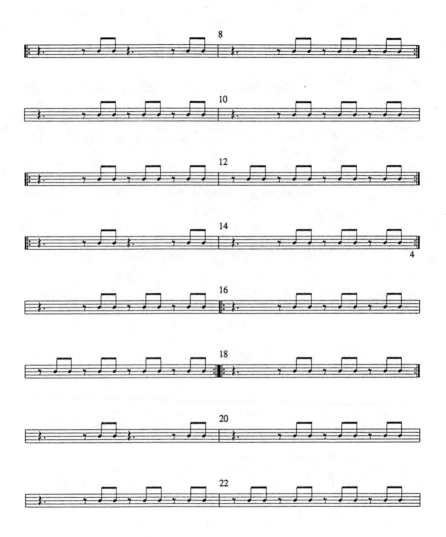

Example 2.4, *continued.*

Example 2.4, *continued.*

Now let's hear the kidi with the bell and the rattle.

Example 2.5 *Gakokoe, axatse, and kidi.*

Example 2.6 *Kidi (axatse marks the beats).*

Now let's hear the bell, the kagan and the kidi sounds together.

Example 2.7 *Gakakoe, kagan, and kidi.*

Example 2.7, *continued.*

Then the master drum which is the kroboto or a bigger drum, the bass drum—sometimes bigger than the kroboto—is used in this case. So let's listen to the master drum also.

Example 2.8 *Gakokoe, axatse, and lead drum.*

Example 2.8, *continued.*

Example 2.8, *continued.*

Example 2.8, *continued.*

Example 2.8, *continued.*

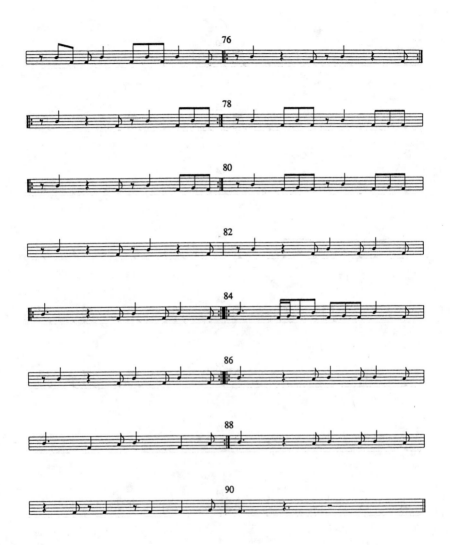

Example 2.8, *continued.*

That is the master drum. Now we will see the combination of the master drum and the kagan and the bell.

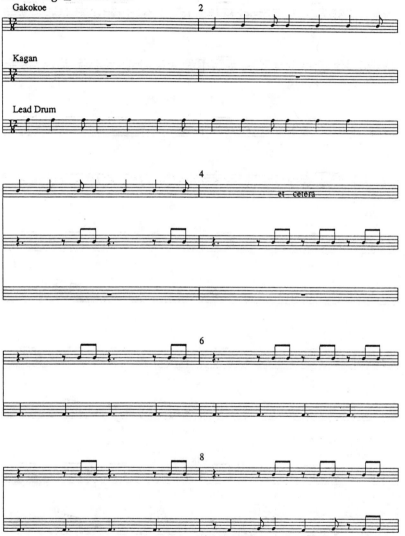

Example 2.9 *Gakakoe, kagan, and lead drum.*

Example 2.9, *continued.*

Example 2.9, *continued.*

Example 2.9, *continued.*

Example 2.9, *continued.*

Example 2.9, *continued.*

Example 2.9, *continued.*

Example 2.9, *continued.*

Example 2.9, *continued.*

The kidi and the master drum.

Example 2.10 *Gakokoe, kidi, and lead drum.*

Example 2.10, *continued.*

Example 2.10, *continued*.

Example 2.10, *continued.*

Example 2.10, *continued.*

Example 2.10, *continued.*

Example 2.10, *continued.*

Example 2.10, *continued.*

Example 2.10, *continued.*

Example 2.10, *continued.*

Example 2.10, *continued.*

Chapter Three

Kpegisu Songs

This chapter contains Ewe texts, English translations, interpretations of meaning, and musical transcriptions of twenty Kpegisu songs. Musically, the lovely tunes and sophisticated rhythms of these songs reward close listening. But unlike the powerful drumming whose excitement radiates immediately across boundaries of history, culture and language, the meaning of Kpegisu songs is more challenging to appreciate.

Vocal music rests firmly within the local Ewe scene. Although it is drumming that first captures the attention of non-Ewe listeners, song texts are "where it is at" if we aspire to an understanding of Kpegisu from the Ewe point of view.[1] Reflecting my intention of maintaining an African voice in this book, Mr. Agbeli's discussion of each song's meaning is presented in a minimally edited version that is quite close to his original words.

The audio and video programs associated with this book enable readers to hear and see performances of these songs. Songs are arranged alphabetically within the categories of Slow Drumming or *Vu Blewu*, Praises or *Ayodede*, and Fast Drumming or *Vutsotsoe*. Chart 3.1 lists the songs by title and shows their classification on the basis of scale mode and form; see Example 6.15 for a summary in musical notation of these tonal features and Chart 6.1 for an outline of the themes and poetic devices in their texts.

Musical Notation

The notation in this chapter is a musical road map, a guide to hearing and performance. The paramount goals are completeness, elegance, and consistency. For this reason, I have omitted analytical markings from these scores. My understanding of how Ewe composers express meaning in song is the subject of Chapter Six.

As is true for the drumming transcriptions, notation cannot be expected to reveal the musical nuances of these songs. Not surprisingly, rhythm offers a significant challenge, a musical puzzle I solve in two ways. First, I write strictly in 12/8 meter because this clearly indicates timing. Even though many vocal rhythms purposely run counter to the unvarying four-feel time, they are grounded firmly within this constant frame of reference. Second, I scrupulously show the timing relationship between each sung tone and the tones in bell phrase. Readers can study the polyrhythm of bell and song by scanning vertically between their two staves. This contrapuntal duet is the key element to a tune's rhythm: If you really understand the potency of the gakokoe rhythm, you can learn to feel the rhythm of a song.

Significant features of the musical notation are listed below:

1. Songs are written in the treble clef with no key signature. Pitch should be regarded as relative, not exact. Songs with the same intervallic relationships among their pitches are transposed to the same pitch set. Intonation as performed is not always identical to the notated pitches; this is discussed in Chapter Six.
2. Rhythm is written in 12/8 meter, but unlike in the drumming scores, ties indicate tones that conspicuously are held over the four-feel beats. Rests indicate active silences.
3. Two-staff systems are used: the gakokoe part in the upper staff, the tune and text in the lower staff. Notes in the two staves are aligned to show graphically the absolutely crucial timing relationship between gakokoe and song.
4. Call-and-response relationships are indicated in bold face letters below the staff in the musical notation and along the left margin of the text, as follows: L for Leader (henọ or song leader), G for Group (hamemegawo or singing group), and A for All (Leader and Group together). (See Chapter One for discussion of the singing group.)
5. In the scores syllables of song text are separated with hyphens; a blend pronounced as one sound between the final vowel of one word and the initial vowel of the next word is indicated with a slash and a hyphen. For example, what is written in the poem as "Adzigo Adzigo" becomes "A-dzi-go/A-dzi-go" in the song text; the rather ugly marking "-go/A-" is pronounced as one sound, that is, "goa."
6. Because of limitations in the score editing software, the Ewe letters not used in English (ɛ, ọ, d, f, ɲ, ʋ, x) are not underlined in the musical transcriptions (see Guide to Typography and Pronuncia-

tion). Please refer to the transcriptions of the Ewe texts and, of
course, the performances by Mr. Agbeli and the Wodome group.

7. As discussed in Chapter Six, the musical form of most songs is
AABBA or AABBCA. In the transcriptions of the song texts, the indication "{2x}" means, "repeat this section twice;" the marking
"{Repeat from the beginning to ★}" means, "repeat from the first
line of text to the star symbol." In the musical transcriptions, first
and second endings are marked conventionally; the reprise of the
opening A section is marked "D.C. al fine," meaning "repeat from
the first double bar to the note under the fermata and Fine indication. It is understood that one song will be repeated several times.
In the performance of the Wodome group, for example, songs
typically are repeated three to five times before another one is
raised.

SLOW DRUMMING (VU BLEWU)

1. Agbeme Nuawo Ken Li	anhemi	E mode	A1A1B1B1 A1
2. Amu Me Dea Dze O	anhemi	E mode	A1 A1 B1B2 C1 A1
3. Donowovi Me Ko Ame O	anhemi	D mode	A1A2 B1B1 C1
4. Gbe Yi Gbe Me Ku La	anhemi	E mode	A1A1 B1B2 A1
5. Gobaya Wo Nye	hemi	B mode	A1A1 B1B2 A1
6. Kadigbe Tsihean	hemi	E mode	A1A1 B1B2 A1
7. Kodzie Ku Ke	anhemi	E mode	A1A2 B1B1 C1
8. Mie Ku Ano Lo		hemi B mode	A1A1 B1B2 C1C2 A1
9. Xe No Ha Mee Me Nye	anhemi	D mode	A1A1 B1B2 C1 A2
10. Yofega Nya Le Vovo De	hemi	B mode	A1A1 B1B2 C1 A1

PRAISES (AYODEDE)

11. Agbemewo Me Si O		hemi B mode	A1A1 B1B1 A1
12. Meli Eku Nava Tso	hemi	B mode	A1A1 B1B2 A1

FAST DRUMMING (VUTSOTSOE)

13. Adzigo Adzigo		hemi B mode	A1A1 B1B2 C1 A2
14. Bo Legbe To	hemi	B mode	A1A1 B1B1 A1
15. Gidigidi Me Wua Kpo O	anhemi	G mode	A1A1 B1B1 A2
16. Kale Nutsu	anhemi	D mode	A1 A2 A3 A4
17. Kpogbale Xoxo	anhemi	D mode	A1 A2 A3 A4
18. Miato Bebeviawo	anhemi	D mode	A1 A2 B1 B2
19. Ne Ho Meli O		anhemi	D mode	A1A1 B1B2 C1 A2
20. Sodegbe Miwo Ge	hemi	B mode	A1A1 B1B2 C1 A2

Chart 3.1 *List of songs in the collection.*

SONG TEXTS

1. AGBEME NUAWO KEN LI

L: 'Gbeme nuawo ken li de.
     Senye metso deke nam o.
     Ye wo se tso hadzidzia de asi nam de.

G: Ha ko madzia, 'Gbodaze gblo be ha ko madzia?
     Eha me nye nu wo du na o de.
     Ma de asie ha ya nua ★ {2x}

L: Mi yo Agbodazewo da

G: Woa xle funyewo nam de.
     Eha me nye nu wo du na o de.
     Ma de asie ha ya nua {2x}

A: {Repeat from beginning to ★}

L: All of life's things are there.
     My destiny gives none to me.
     My destiny puts singing in my hands.

G: "Is it only song I will sing," *Agbodaze* says,
     "Is it only song I will sing?"
     Song is not a thing that can be eaten.
     Can I release this song from my hand? ★ {2x}

L: You (pl.) call over to *Agbodaze*

G: To count my sufferings for me.
     Song is not a thing that can be eaten.
     Can I release this song from my hand? {2x}

A: {Repeat from beginning to ★ }

In this song the singer blames Destiny (*Se*) for making him a composer.[2] When you sing you gain nothing, only problems (ritual obligations, social duties). People ask you to sing about their problems but will give you only drink for your efforts. And at your funeral, who will sing? Destiny could have given him many things, but his was to be a poor composer. *Agbodaze* could be a drinking nickname (*ahanonko*).

2. AMU ME DEA DZE O

L: Amu me dea dze o lo.
     Tumfo be yea de dze de.

G: Aho dze aho dzi Bluawo yi de magbo he. ★ {2x}
L: Tumfoe gblo na viawo be,
G: Miva mi de dze le amu me a. ★ {2x}
A: Ye wo be Kodzaledzie tsi amu me.
      Kodzaledzie tso mo na Kpogo,
      Be Kodzaledzie tsi amu me tegbe.
      {Repeat from beginning to ★}

L: A river does not produce salt.
      The *Akan* chief says he wants to collect salt.
G: When the sun rose the *Akans* went and never returned. ★ {2x}
L: The *Akan* chief told his warriors,
G: "Come and let's collect salt from the river." {2x}
A: And they said, "*Kodzaledzi* drowned in the river.
      Kodzaledzi who crossed the road for Kpogo,
      Kodzaledzi is drowned forever."
      {Repeat from beginning to ★}

Salt is not found in the Akan area but the Akans know the Ewes get salt from water. The Akan chief asks his own people to imitate the Ewes and try to get salt from their rivers. The Ewes are mocking the Akans for trying something which can never work. Then they got the news that in this activity their great enemy, *Kodzaledzie,* had drowned. At the same time they are poking fun at the Akans they are praising him.

Mr. Agbeli accepts my interpretation that this song compares the impossibility of getting salt from a river with the likelihood that the Akans can defeat the Ewes.[3] Salt is a symbol for the Ewes and river for the Akans. The song implies a battle between the two with the Akans defeated, their champion killed. *Yofega Nya le Vovo De* (song 10) also makes references to warfare between the Ewe and the Akan.

3. DONOWOVI ME KO AME O

L: Dogbeto be donowovi me ko ame o lo.
G: Donowovi me ko ame o. {2x}
A: Wo ha donowovie ne nye.
      Nye ha donowovie me nye.
      Dogbeto be mega ko nu nade tsitsi de me o.
      Dawoto ya de wo kade me nea?
      Donowovi me ko ame o lo he.

L: Dogbeto said, "A sick person's child does not laugh at a person."
G: A sick person's child does not laugh at a person. {2x}
A: You are also a sick person's child.
      I am also a sick person's child.
      Dogbeto said, "Don't laugh and remove the eyeglasses.
      Has your mother's [sickness] become better?"
      A sick person's child does not laugh at a person.

This is a moralistic song whose message is, "We all have problems, so we should not laugh at others. Someday the problems we laugh at will be our own." The metaphor used is sickness, in this case of one's own mother. One should not laugh (even so hard as to weep and need to wipe our eyes) because, after all, your own mother is suffering as well.

4. GBE YI GBE ME KU LA

L: Gbe yi gbe me ku la.
      Kosi be miga kom ade zavu ne mia di o,
G: Dakpo na no ta nama.
      Ye dilawo mi ga nlom be de o he.
      Du nku na kpo mia wo o. ★ {2x}
L: Sakpate wo ku ame wum he.
G: Deviwo kua wo nublanuia. {2x}
A: {Repeat from beginning to ★}

L: The day that I die.
      Kosi says, "Don't carry me into a night lorry to bury,
G: My head to remain partly shaved.
      My buryers, don't forget me alone
      For the town's eye to look at us." ★ {2x}
L: The smallpox death is killing people.
G: Children's death is miserable. {2x}
A: {Repeat from beginning to ★}

This song is about a bad death, that is, a death from sickness, physical injury, or accident. It is believed that such deaths are caused by a violation of the proper ways-of-living. Infractions may cause gods such as *Sakpate* to bring a bad death to a household. In such cases, the burial must be made in the night and without certain rites. For example, the head will not be shaved and the hair and nails will not be saved for a second burial and honorific memorial service. This makes it plain that the death is unwanted. The spirit of the deceased will not reincarnate and continue the misfortune within the family.

In this song the composer pleads not to suffer a bad death. He does not want to be buried in the night, with his head partly shaved, left alone for the townspeople to observe and his family to be disgraced.

5. GQBAYA WO NYE

L: Gǫbaya wo nye matsǫe matsǫ ta yi yǫme de.
G: Danyevi dǫ koa ne anyi nam he.
Gǫbaya wo nye ne me dǫ nue dzivǫwo dza gbe de.
Matsǫe matsǫ ta yi yǫme. ★ {2x}
L: Ale yi mawǫ na dumegawo he
G: Du nkuwo ma ga kpǫm o a?
L: Ale yi mawǫ na dumegawo
G: Du nkuwo ma ga kpǫm o a?
A: {Repeat from beginning to ★}

L: He is the Agobin leaf I will take to cover my head to go to the place of the dead.
G: My poor brother should stay [alive] for me.
He is the Agobin leaf, when I remember the day of the bad rains.
I will take it to cover my head to go to the place of the dead. ★ {2x}
L: What shall I do for the big men of the town
G: So that the eyes of the town cannot see me? {2x}
A: {Repeat from beginning to ★}

The song is in two parts. The first part emphasizes that family is one's shelter in life and in death. Your siblings can never be forgotten, disregarded or ignored; unlike a friend they will always be involved in your life. The *Agǫbin* tree is a very tall palm whose frond makes an excellent shelter and umbrella. Thus, the brother or sister is likened to this powerful image. In the song's second part the composer wonders what he can do so that important people will know and respect him. He implies that whatever one does—whether good or bad—people will still gossip about you. When he says, "So that the eyes of the town cannot see me," he means, "So that I will not be ashamed, or disgraced." Taken together, the two parts of the song mean:

there is nothing I can do for the townspeople so that they will love me like my own family.

6. KADIGBE TSIHE

L: Kadigbe tsihe mele miawo si o. {2x}
      Be vivime koe me tsi de.

G: Nugbe mayia ne mayi yevuwo de he
      Ne masi gomekadi mada di he.
      Makpo ngonye mayi tsie he. ★ {2x}

A: Dogbeto be yawo fa mee mele de.
      Madi dokuinye le agbe me. {2x}
      {Repeat from beginning to ★}

L: We don't have a lamp carrier. {2x}
      We are in darkness.

G: I have to travel, to go to the white man's country
      To light the lantern and put it down.
      I look forward to go to the land of the dead. ★ {2x}

A: Dogbeto says, "This is what I am mourning for.
      I should bury myself while I am alive." {2x}
      {Repeat from beginning to ★}

The lamp or lantern is a traditional type, either a tin can with a wick as seen in the Wodome video, or, even more traditionally, a pottery bowl full of palm oil with a rag wick. The carrier is a cloth wrapped into a circular shape and placed on the head as a padding.

The carrier stands for wealth. The song refers to the poverty of the singer. The white man's country can mean going overseas, to the modern city, or simply to a wealthy person who can pay good wages. Lighting the lantern means getting money; putting it down means to use the money. *Dogbeto* is announcing that these are his needs so that he can live well in life, and/or make the necessary preparations for his death. "Bury myself while I am alive" means to amass a savings for use in his burial, or more generally, to be a generous person so that many people will come and help make one's funeral grand. The song urges people to do things in life that will yield a fitting burial, especially to join a funeral group and pay proper dues.

7. KODZIE KU KE

L: Kodzie ku ke de amewo dzie.
G: Aba konua be av̱lime av̱limea,
    Gbǫgbǫa zu dǫe. {2x}
A: Mile nǫvisia!
    Kpegi fotǫ be mile nǫvisia! {2x}
    Ye wo be agbe nǫ kaka gbe
    Yǫme ade meli o he.
    Yǫme nye afe.

L: The hoe put sand on people.
G: The mat laughed and said, "The land of the dead,
    Coming back is difficult." {2x}
A: Be united!
    The Kpegisu player says, "Be united!"
    And they say, "Long life without death can never be.
    The place of the dead is home."

When a person dies he or she is laid in state on mat, but when it is a bad death the body is buried with the mat. The "laughing mat" is a metaphor for a person who laughs at another's problems; the singer is saying that these problems could easily happen to you, so you shouldn't laugh at others. On the contrary, we should be united. Rich or poor we should all be in brotherhood because we all end at the same place, the place of the dead. Death is final; coming back from the dead—it can never be.

8. MIE KU ANO LO

L: Mie ku anǫ lo. Devie nye de.
G: Fonyemeawo de be mie ku anǫ lo. Devie nye de. ★ {2x}
L: Mikpǫ kukuawo nam da lo.
G: Gbagbeawo ha gbǫna.
L: Mikpǫ kukuawo nam da.
G: Gbagbeawo ha gbǫna.
A: Fonyemeawo de awǫ num alea be nku nye adze tsieawo dzi. {2x}
    {Repeat from beginning to ★}

L: You are greedy. The townchild is the one who builds the town.

G: My family, I say, "You are greedy. The townchild is the one who builds the town." {2x}
L: Look at the dead ones for me.
G: The living ones are also coming. {2x}
A: My family has done this to me and I remember the dead. {2x}
      {Repeat from beginning to ★}

A song of complaint towards the composer's family. His extended family is greedy and gives him no help. Even his ancestors were greedy and now the living ones are continuing the same way. Though it is bad ettiquette to mention the dead, the actions of the living have forced him to do it. Anyone who hears the song should re-evaluate his behavior.

9. XE NǪ HA MEE ME NYE

L: Xe nǫ ha mee me nye he.
      Ye wo be nye me ku na dǫ wo ku o he.
G: Xe nǫ ha mee me nye he.
      Ye wo be nye me ku na dǫ wo ku o. {2x}
L: Papayesue gblǫm be,
G: Gbǫsusua nu nyuie adee. {2x}
A: Nake gblǫm be nye deka koe danye dzia.
      Nye deka koe nye duawo nǫvi.
      Be naneke ya me wǫm o.
      Xe nǫ ha mee me nye he.
      Ye wo be nye me ku na dǫ wo ku o.

L: I am a bird inside a group.
      And they say I will never die from sickness.
G: {Repeat leader's text} {2x}
L: Hawk is saying that
G: To be many is a good thing. {2x}
A: *Nake* is saying that I am the only issue of my mother.
      I am the only brother of the townspeople.
      So nothing happens to me.
      I am a bird inside a group.
      And they say I will never die from sickness.

The song's basic message is that a generous-spirited member of a group will be protected by friends and never suffer. The image of birds helps convey the meaning. Membership in a drumming and dancing society is compared to being a bird in a flock. The solitary hawk comments on the advantages of a more social way of living. Even though the singer is an only child, through his helpful ways all the townspeople have become like family to him. The named person, *Nake*, could be the composer or the one to whom the song is dedicated. Song's often are composed as a way of enhancing the reputation of someone who has helped the composer. Songs also can be used to criticize or to ask forgiveness.

10. YOFEGA NYA LE VOVO DE

L: Yofega nya le vovo de.
      Bluawo de dzie domea koyi afee.
G: Danyi de Yofega nya le vovo ha.
      Bluawo de dzie domea he ★ {2x}
L: Devie menye de.
G: Mekpo nuawo ken tefe. {2x}
A: Gbemagbea mie do de datu la.
      Yaluvi kponue Bedzamoa be do.
      Nye kple Bluawo mi no dudia kema.
      Wo do tefe de me megbe yi ge mia lae.
      {Repeat from ' then from beginning to }

L: The story of *Yofega* is different.
      The *Akans* took the heart from his stomach to their home.
G: *Danyi*, the story of *Yofega* is different.
      The *Akans* took the heart from his stomach. {2x}
L: ' I am a child.
G: I have seen the place of everything. {2x}
A: That day we met at *Datu*
      Bedzamo was hiding at *Yaluvi's* fence.
      I was competing with the *Akans*.
      When it reaches the climax, is it not backwards that you must go?
      {Repeat from ' and then from beginning to }

This song concerns a heated discussion about their forefathers between the singer and his antagonist, *Danyi*. The singer remembers that when he was a child there was a fight between the *Ewe* and the *Akan*. The Akans killed the singer's brave ancestor, *Yofega*, but Danyi's forefather, *Bedzamo*, was a coward. He hid at *Yaluvi's* fence and ran away at the climax of the battle. The song also teaches the moral that one should go ahead strongly in any activity, no matter what the consequences.

11. AGBEMEWO ME SI O

L: Me do leli agbemewo me si nam o he. {2x}
    Ye wo be ame ble na he.

G: Ahablutsie ahame wo dọ na ḏo.
    Dọgbetọ me si o.
    Sogbo be ahablustie ahame wo dọ na ḏo. {2x}

L: Dọgbetọ ḏọ Sowu ḏe.

G: Ne gbọ ne gbọ he.
    Ne agbenu ade li mia wọ. {2x}

A: {Repeat from beginning to }

L: I shouted [but] the living did not hear me. {2x}
    And they said people get lost.

G: The stirring stick dissolves in the drink.
    Dọgbetọ did not hear it.
    Sogbo said, "The stirring stick dissolves in the drink." {2x}

L: *Dọgetọ* sent a person to *Sowu*.

G: He should come, he should come
    If there is something for us to do in life, we do it. {2x}

A: {Repeat from beginning to }

A song about the origin of Kpegisu. *Dọgbetọ's* brother, *Sowu*, often went deep into the forest and one day got lost. He shouted but they, the living people, could not hear him. (The implication is that he had been bewitched by the dwarfs of the forest.) Dọgbetọ sent people out, calling for him to come back so that they could accomplish whatever they should do in life as brothers. When Sowu returned, he showed Dọgbetọ the drumming and dancing that the dwarfs were doing. Dọgbetọ composed a song about the incident and Kpegisu was born. In this, his first song, he tells the story of origin.

12. *ME LI EKU NA VA TSǪ*

L: Me li eku na va tsǫ.
   Dǫgbetǫ be me li eku na va tsǫe.
G: Hae haee, me ga yǫ nam o.
   Me li eku na va tsǫe. {2x}
L :'Mega 'megawo na nǫ anyi ɖe he.
G: Wo ava gblǫe nam ma dzudzǫa? {2x}
A: {Repeat from beginning to }

L: I live for death to come and take me.
   Dǫgbetǫ said, "I live for death to come and take me."
G: It is a song, it is a song, don't rush me.
   I live for death to come and take me. {2x}
L: The elders should come and sit.
G: Can they come to tell me to rest? {2x}
A: {Repeat from beginning to }

A song about being a composer. Despite his many hardships, the composer Dǫgbetǫ says that he will sing and wait for death to come and take him. Although important people advise him to stop, he will sing, sing, and not be dissuaded. He knows what he is doing and will accept the consequences of what will happen in his life. No one should pity him.

Why does composing bring suffering? When you are concentrating on songs you will not put your efforts into rewarding work. As the proverb says, "The composer's farm is always weedy." You will compose against people who will not be pleased and may make trouble for you. For example, if you compose against a person, he may retaliate by invoking gods who will come to you and insist that you become their priest and provide expensive sacrifices. Composers often are the priests of many gods and are required to spend heavily.

Men often become composers because one of their forefathers had made *akaya*, the charm for singers. The man will be visited in his dreams by this ancestor and/or will behave as if "possessed" by the need to sing. Then his family will know that he must make the sacrifices and herbal preparations of akaya for himself and lead the troubled life of composer.

This song refers to the history of Kpegisu, itself. It is likely that Dǫgbetǫ is the brother of *Sowu*, the man who got lost in the forest and brought Kpegisu back from the dwarfs.

13. ADZIGO ADZIGO

L: Adzigo Adzigo so ɖe gbe miawo nua.
G: Anlɔwo be Adzigo Adzigo so ɖe gbe miawo nua. {2x}
L: Anlɔwo tsɔ tu,
G: Tsɔ tu yi aʋa wɔ ge.
L: Anlɔwo tsɔ yi,
G: Tsɔ yi yi aʋa wɔ ge.
A: Aʋa wɔ nutsu ya me sia ku o lo.
       So ɖe gbe miawo nua.
       Anlɔwo be Adzigo Adzigo so ɖe gbe miawo nua.

L: Adzigo Adzigo—on the day of the fighting we will do the thing.
G: The Anlɔs say, "Adzigo Adzigo—on the day of the fighting we
       will do the thing. {2x}
L: The Anlɔs take guns,
G: Take guns and go to war.
L: The Anlɔs take swords,
G: Take swords and go to war.
A: A warrior does not fear death.
       On the day of the fighting we will do the thing.
       The Anlɔs say, "Adzigo Adzigo—on the day of the fighting
       we will do the thing.

Adzigo is a village in Togo. The Anlɔ warriors are stating directly their
intention to go and fight bravely.

14. BO LEGBE TO

L: Bɔ legbe tɔ me dia nu do kpo o.
       Yeku dze Abla me.
G: {Repeat leader's text} {2x}
L: Yeku dze Abla me lo.
G: Yeku dze Abla me. {2x}
A: {Repeat to }

L: A long-armed person does not search and fail.
       Yeku gets into Abla.
G: {Repeat leader's text} {2x}

L: Yeku gets into Abla [announcing].
     Yeku gets into Abla.
A: {Repeat to }

This is an *Afa* song. In its most literal meaning, the song is about someone who is searching or seeking for something and has consulted an Afa
priest. *Yeku* and *Abla* are names of divinations in Afa. This casting indicates
that he will get what he wants, provided he has performed the proper rites.
Castings are termed "broken" or "straight." A "straight" casting means that
the supplicant already is a "long-armed" person (that is, a generous person);
if it is "broken" the person must perform some Afa rites.

The song also speaks to life in general. It means that people can get
whatever they want in life provided they are willing to do what is necessary.
Especially, you have to expand your contacts with people, be open-hearted
and helpful. The "long arm" image is equivalent to "extending a helping
hand to others."

15. GIDIGIDI ME WUA KPO O

L: Gidigidi me wua kpo o.
     Kpo la wu gbe ada do me.
G: Gidigi me wua kpo o.
     Kpo wu gbe ada do. {2x}
L: Tua wui lo.
G: Iye!
L: Tua wui lo.
G: Iye ha!
     Tua wui de adzido gome.
     'Meka be vie ma yo? {2x}
A: {Repeat from beginning to }

L: Rushing does not kill the leopard.
     On the day of killing the leopard, there should be seriousness.
G: {Repeat leader's text} {2x}
L: The gun has killed it.
G: Indeed!
L: The gun has killed it.
G: Indeed!

> The gun has killed it under the baobub tree.
> Whose child shall I call? {2x}
> A: {Repeat from beginning to }

The dangerous hunt for a leopard stands as a metaphor for any important task a person may undertake. When a hunter seeks to kill a leopard, he should plan well, take time, and act with a cool mind. And when the time comes for action, he must do it properly because he could lose his life. Similarly, serious work should be planned well and carried out with seriousness. The song confirms that this is the key to the hunter's success. The baobub tree symbolizes the hunter's proper planning and execution. The pleased hunter wants to announce his victory to others, saying "Whose child shall I call?"

16. KALE NUTSU

L: Kale nutsu agbadza dze wo he.
G: Kale vava. {2x}
L: Kale nutsu agbadza dze wo.
G: Kale vava.
A: Kale nutsu agbadza dze wo he.
       Kale vava.

L: Warrior, the war belt really fits you.
G: True warrior. {2x}
L: Warrior, the war belt fits you.
G: True warrior.
A: Warrior, the war belt really fits you.
       True warrior.

Like *Adzigo Adzigo*, this song speaks directly about war. The man clearly is suited to be a warrior, he likes the work, he is ready to do it.

17. KPOGBALE XOXO

L: Kpogbale xoxoa le tsi gbe tsie fo.
G: Nonoea vo wo nue. {2x}
A: Kpogbale xoxoa le tsi gbe tsie fo.
       Nonoea vo wo nue. {2x}

L: The old leopard skin is left for the rain to beat.
G: The spots are gone. {2x}
A: {Repeat all} {2x}

This song is a proverb. The leopard skin refers to someone who had done many great things earlier in his or her lifetime. The rain means that the person has been defeated by another person, or otherwise has come upon hard times. The spots being gone means that the person is no longer as great as before, he or she has become a common person like everyone else. The Ewes believe that the rich will not always be rich, the poor not always poor. Things even out. Another relevant proverb says, "A woman's breast, so beautiful in youth, inevitably will fall."

18. MIATQ BEBEVIAWO

L: Miatǫ Bebviawo,
G: Nua mele vivm o.{2x}
A: Nyabada nuglo nyae dzǫ.
       Enuglo nyae dzǫ.

L: Fellow friends of *Bebe*,
G: The thing is not sweet. {2x}
A: Bad word, everyone is tired.
       Everyone is tired.

Bebe refers to Benin Beer, which is brewed in Togo. When this local brand of beer was first introduced in Togo in the early 1960's it became very popular: people made special trips from Ghana to Togo to drink, performing groups took the name Bebe, and people even named their children Bebe.

The song is a way for the performers to tell the elders that they are tired and need drink. This type of song is not sung with too much repetition because the people really want the elders to know that they need refreshment. The song is appropriate for the *Adzo* sections of the fast drumming; after it is sung the song leader will cue the ending. The elders should know that if drink is not brought, the group will take a full break and destroy the momentum of the performance.

19. NE HQ ME LI O

L: Mi woe mi woe!
       Ne hǫ me li o, fia la nya du ha?
       Mi woe mi woe!

Ne hǫ me li o, fia la nya ḏu.
G: {Repeat Leader's text} {2x}
L: Me wǫ nyo na mi gbaḏegbe he.
G: Akpe me le 'me wo xǫ na o. {2x}
A: Vatsakpolie gblǫm be,
     Mi le hǫ mia wu he.
     Ne hǫ me li o fia la nya ḏu ha?
     {Repeat from beginning to }

L: You (pl.) do it, you do it!
     If the eagle is not there, can the chief be enstooled?
     [repeat]
G: {Repeat Leader's text} {2x}
L: I did good for you (pl.) some day.
G: They receive without thanks {2x}
A: *Vatsakpoli* says,
     "Catch the eagle and kill it."
     If the eagle is not there, can the chief be enstooled?
     {Repeat from beginning to }

This is a story from an *Afa* divination. Eagle was made chief with the power to catch and eat all the other birds. *Vatsakpoli* (a bird that flies in a flock) was the stool-owner *(zikpuitǫ)* with the right to govern when Eagle was away, and the authority of approving a new chief. Knowing his power, Eagle always ate Vatsakpoli's children. At last Vatsakpoli gathered all the birds and advised them to kill Eagle because he was eating their children. He argued that he had done many good deeds for Eagle, such as making him chief, but Eagle had never thanked him. The birds asked, "If Eagle is not there, can a chief be made?" Vatsakpoli replied, "Yes, since I am stool-owner, a new chief can be enstooled."

The song teaches a moral: if someone has done good for you, you should try and thank the person. Even though Vatsakpoli made Eagle chief, Eagle always ate his children. A second lesson is that leaders should not abuse their power. Eagle was seeking complete power even though custom dictates that chiefs must work together with the stool-owner and other elders. For example, sacrifices to the stool cannot be done without the stool-owner being present and if something good comes to the stool, it is the stool-owner who receives the greater share. The office of chieftancy has a division of power.

20. *SODEGBE MI WO GE*

L: Da tum de ne sodebe mi wo ge.
G: Amewo da tum de ne sodegbe mi wo ge. {2x}
L: Amewo tso tu.
G: Tso tu yi ava wo ge.
L: Amewo tso yi.
G: Tso yi yi ava wo ge.
A: Ava wo nutsu ya me sia tu o de.
      Be sodegbe mi wo ge.
      Amewo da tum de ne sodegbe mi wo ge.

L   :[You] shot me with gun, on the fighting day we shall do it.
G: People shot me with gun, on the fighting day we shall do it. {2x}
L: People take guns.
G: Take guns and go to make war.
L: People take cutlasses.
G: Take cutlases and go to make war.
A: A true warrior never fears gun.
      On the fighting day, we shall do it.
      People shot me with gun, on the fighting day we shall do it.

The song voices the perspective of a combatant against an enemy, very likely an enemy within his own group. The song's voice says, "You have offended me, but I will not take it seriously now. But when it comes to the appropriate time, we shall all see what the result will be. Yes, you have succeeded in doing things to me today, but I will not reply now because I do not fear anything. I know how to respond but I only keep quiet for now."

SONG SCORES

AGBEME NUAWO KEN LI

m de   E- ha me nye nu/wo du   na/o de   Ma de/a -sie   ha

ya nua   **L:** Mi yo/A -gbo-da-dze/wo   da   **G:** Woa xle   fu -nyewo na-

m de   E- ha me nye nu/wo du   na/o de   Ma de/a -sie   ha

D.C. al fine

ya nua   **A:** 'Gbe -me nuawo ken wo li

AMU ME DEA DZE O

DONOWOVI ME KO AME O

L: Do- gbe -to be do-no-wo-vi me ko/a - me/o lo　　G: Do-no-wo-vi me ko/a -

me/o　　　　　　　　　　　　　　L: Do- gbe -to be do-no-wo-vi me ko/a -

me/o lo　　G: Do-no-wo-vi me ko/a - me/o　　A: Wo ha　Do-no-wo-vie　ne

nye　Nye ha　do-no-wo-vie　me　nye　Do-gbe -to be me-ga ko nu na-de

tsi -tsi de me/o　Da-wo-to ya de/wo ka-de me nea　Do-no-wo-vi me ko/a -

⌢ Fine

GBE YI GBE ME KU LA

GOBAYA WO NYE

KADIGBE TSIHE

KODZIE KU KE

L: Ko-dzie ku ke de/a -me- wo dzie   G: A- ba ko-nua be/a -

vli -me/a -vli -mea   Gbo-gboa zu doe

L: Ko-dzie ku ke de/a -me- wo dzie   G: A- ba ko-nua be/a -

vli -me/a -vli -mea   Gbo-gboa zu doe   A: Mi-le no-vi -

sia   Kpe-gi fo -to be mi-le no-vi - sia   Mi-le no-vi -

sia   Kpe-gi fo -to be mi-le no-vi - sia   Ye wo be/a -gbe no ka -ka gbe

Fine

Yo-me/a -de me li/o   he   Yo-me nye/a -fe oo

MIE KU ANO LO

XE NO HA MEE ME NYE

♩.= 96

1
L: Xe no ha mee me nye he Ye wo be nye me ku na do

3
wo ku o he G: Xe no ha mee me nye he Ye wo be nye me ku na do

1. 2.

5
wo ku o L: Xe no ha mee me wo ku o L: Pa-pa- ye-sue gblo -

7
m be G: Gbo-su-sua nu nyuie/a -dee L: Pa-pa- ye-sue gblo -

9
m be G: Gbo-su-sua nu nyuie/a - dee A: Na-ke gblo -

11
m be nye de-ka ko-e da-nye dzia Nye de-ka ko-e nye

13
dua-wo no-vi Be na-ne-ke ya me wom o Xe no ha mee me

Fine

15
nye he Ye wo be nye me ku na do wo ku o

YOFEGA NYA LE VOVO DE

AGBEMEWO ME SI O

ME LI EKU NAVA TSO

ADZIGO ADZIGO

L: A- dzi -go/A- dzi -go so de

gbe mia-wo nua G: An-lo -wo be/A- dzi -go/A- dzi - go so de

gbe mia-wo nua L: A- gbe mia-wo nua L: An-lo -wo tso

tu G: Tso tu yi/a -va wo ge L: An-lo -wo tso

yi G: Tso yi yi/a - va wo ge A: A- va wo nu- tsu ya me

sia ku o lo So de gbe mia-wo nua An-lo -wo be/A -

Fine

dzi -go/A- dzi -go so de gbe mia-wo nua

BO LEGBE TO

GIDIGIDI ME WUA KPO O

KALE NUTSU

KPOGBALE XOXO

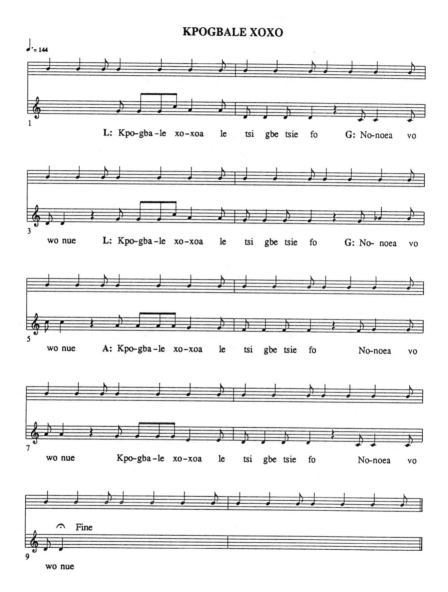

L: Kpo-gba-le xo-xoa le tsi gbe tsie fo   G: No-noea vo

wo nue   L: Kpo-gba-le xo-xoa le tsi gbe tsie fo   G: No- noea vo

wo nue   A: Kpo-gba-le xo-xoa le tsi gbe tsie fo   No-noea vo

wo nue   Kpo-gba-le xo-xoa le tsi gbe tsie fo   No-noea vo

Fine

wo nue

MIATO BEBEVIAWO

NE HO ME LI O

SODEGBE MI WO GE

Chapter Four

The Percussion Ensemble

*T*his chapter presents the percussion ensemble music for Kpegisu. We include the gakokoe part, meter, and the rhythm of each instrument in the ensemble.

Ewe drummers prefer not to talk about drumming in technical terms, but I believe the views presented here are consistent with Ewe musical thought. My way of thinking and talking about Ewe music has developed over a long period of apprenticeship, performance, and scholarship.[1]

Tempo

Given that this is music for dance, it is not surprising that a steady unchanging tempo is the norm for Kpegisu. Despite the musical effects of polyrhythm and cross rhythm, competent Ewe musicians maintain their time with ease. Not all Ewes are musically adept, however. Non-Africans are not the only ones who "go off," that is, play with unsteady tempo. Mr. Agbeli's presentations are all at one moderately fast tempo (dotted-quarter = 130); the Wodome group has sections in slow and fast tempi (dotted-quarter = 118 and 156); when Mr. Agbeli sang the Wodome songs for the audio program he chose a slower pace (dotted-quarter = 96 and 140). The following discussion is based on Mr. Agbeli's demonstration.

Gakokoe

Repetition is the life blood of this music. As parts repeat, the shape of musical time becomes circular or spiral. The ensemble's polyrhythm is stable yet ever-changing and at its heart, repeating over-and-over without variation, is the gakokoe. Ewe teachers always emphasize its importance. All performance arts—drumming, singing, dancing—are timed in duet with its recurring phrase. Its rhythm inspires the design of the other parts and the duet with the gakokoe is crucial to their musical effectiveness. At first it may seem a simple thing but as the discussion will show, the bell phrase can support a lifetime of musical exploration.

Bell tones are of two durations, short and long, represented in notation by eighth and quarter notes. One complete unit of the gakokoe phrase requires seven strokes but Ewe musicians, I am convinced, never count bell strokes. They *feel* the music's flow and *hear* the interaction of rhythmic shapes. For analytical and pedagogical purposes, I will use the following numbering scheme (see Example 4.1).

Example 4.1
Gakokoe phrase as seven long and short tones.

Inexorably repeating in a polyrhythmic context, these seven tones form and reform into different configurations which we can term **modes of the gakokoe phrase**.[2] The gakokoe part seems to change depending on how the tones are grouped into phrases. Adept musicians easily maintain tempo and polyphonic alignment, but inexperienced players may be confused by these *perceived* reconfigurations.[3] Although seven gakokoe tones can generate an unlimited number of patterns, the following modes are significant in my analysis of Mr. Agbeli's presentation of Kpegisu (see Example 4.2).

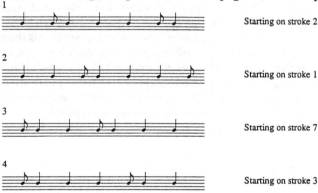

Example 4.2 *Modes of the gakokoe phrase.*

Configurations 1 and 2 are the most important ways of hearing the gakokoe phrase. This is how the part is presented by Ewe teachers. I have drawn attention to the other patterns because of the interactive influence of other instruments in the ensemble. The lead drum part, for example, often places accentuation on gakokoe stroke 7, hence the importance of mode 3; the kagan part brings mode 4 into acoustic prominence.

Pulsation And Beats

Implicit to the gakokoe phrase is a steady flow of musical time. The bell's seven strokes occur within a grid of twelve equal units of time—the eighth note pulse (see Example 4.3).

12 eighths per gakokoe phrase

Gakokoe phrase

Example 4.3 *Eighth note pulse and the gakokoe phrase.*

These twelve eighth notes are felt in terms of two longer time units: 1) beats containing three partials (dotted-quarters), and 2) beats containing two partials (quarter notes). Four ternary beats and six binary beats occur within the time span of the gakokoe phrase. Frequently, the two beat "feels" are combined into a three-then-two pattern (see Example 4.4). As seen in the Wodome video, singers often clap hands in 4-beat, 6-beat, or 3-then-2 time.

Two other equidurational units of time are important in this theory: sixteenths and dotted-eighths. The subdivision of the eighth note pulse into a faster sixteenth note pulse (twenty four per gakokoe phrase) primarily is theoretical; that is, it never is played except briefly in the lead drum part. On the other hand, the 8-beat feel (dotted-eighths) is vitally important. Dotted-eighths subdivide dotted-quarters, establish intense cross rhythm (2:3 with eighths, 4:3 with quarters), and create exciting polyrhythm with the gakokoe.

4-beat feel: each beat contains three pulses

6-beat feel: each beat contains two pulses

3-then-2 feel

Example 4.4
Beats within the time span of the gakokoe phrase.

Fast pulse

Eight feel

Example 4.5 *Sixteenth note pulses and the 8-beat feel.*

Meter

The gakokoe phrase can be heard in 4-beat, 6-beat, 3-then-2, and 8-beat feels. As the feeling of beat changes, the listener's perception of the gakokoe phrase also may shift. In Example 4.6 beams and ties visually represent the perceived reconfiguration of the gakokoe rhythm.

Thus far, I have suggested two sources for musical depth in the gakokoe phrase: 1) grouping and re-grouping the seven tones into a variety of phrases, and 2) changing the "ground" (beats or metric stresses) in terms of which the "figure" (gakokoe phrase) is perceived. The gakokoe phrase may be compared to a work of visual or plastic art—a sculpture, a mobile, or a gemstone. The moments in time when the wooden stick strikes the iron bell never change, but their musical effect is dynamic. Creativity in melodic

Gakokoe in four

Gakokoe in six

Gakokoe in 3-2

Gakokoe in eight

Example 4.6
Gakokoe phrase in 4-beat, 6-beat, 3-2, and 8-beat meters.

composition, dance variations, or lead drumming depends upon a keen appreciation of the manifold potential of the gakokoe.

This quality, which might be called rhythmic multideterminancy, should not be over-emphasized, however. There is one interpretation of the time that is more basic or fundamental; the others are secondary or countermetric. Ewe musicians, I am convinced, hear the gakokoe "in four."[4]

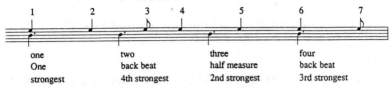

1	2	3 '4	5	6	7
one	two	three	four		
One	back beat	half measure	back beat		
strongest	4th strongest	2nd strongest	3rd strongest		

Example 4.7 *Stress pattern in 4-beat meter.*

The moment of articulated and felt musical resolution is beat one, stroke 1. Beat three carries the second strongest stress. This is readily apparent in the way people clap on beats one and three during the songs interlude section (Hatsiatsia) of the Wodome performance. Furthermore, many song phrases begin at the mid-point of the gakokoe phrase and move towards cadence on beat one. Beat four is special because it occurs in unison with gakokoe stroke 6; coming after the offbeat strokes 2-5, stroke 6 marks the convergence of 4-beat feel and gakokoe phrase, foreshadowing the cadence on beat one. Beat two carries the weakest inherent stress. One final point: given the metric emphasis on beats one and three, beats two and four often acquire prominence as "backbeats." Some readers may react skeptically to this analysis because it seems surprisingly similar to a Western 12/8 meter. According to my experience, however, it is "in the music."

Offbeating and Cross Rhythm

The 4-beat and 6-beat interpretations of the gakokoe phrase are givens in Ewe music. Musicians create rhythmic excitement by playing off the beat. Some rhythms dart from onbeat to offbeat positions—the gakokoe is an example—but offbeating also can follow regular and consistent patterns. In a relatively simple way, beats two and four are the recurring offbeats of beats one and three. Offbeats also occur at the speed of the eighth note pulse. In these materials on Kpegisu, Mr. Agbeli consistently accentuates the "ands" of the 6-beat meter (the upbeat 6-feel) and the third partial of each 4-feel beat.

Example 4.8 *Consistent offbeats.*

The upbeat 6-feel is vital in the lead drum part. It is interesting to realize that the gakokoe phrase may be understood as a combination of the onbeat 6-feel and upbeat 6-feel. Strokes 1-3 manifest the onbeat, strokes 4-7 sound out the upbeat.

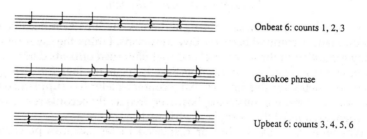

Example 4.9 *Gakokoe phrase and the 6-beat meters.*

Cross rhythm is a special type of offbeating. In Kpegisu as presented by Mr. Agbeli, 3:2 is by far the most important type of cross rhythm. "Three-in-the-space-of-two" happens between both the onbeat and upbeat 6-feels and the beats of the 4-feel. Notice that the moment of simultaneity between the upbeat 6-feel and the 4-feel is on beats two and four, thus lending further weight to the backbeats. Cross rhythmic drum phrases can begin on the moment of simultaneity with the 4-feel beats, but more commonly are phrased two-three-one and sometimes three-one-two.

Example 4.10   *Cross rhythm.*

It is doubtful that these offbeats and cross rhythms ever become the predominant perceptual basis for Ewe musicians. I think the Ewes remain firmly grounded in the 4-beat feel and that patterned offbeats derive their power from this fixed way of hearing. Strictly speaking, therefore, Kpegisu is not polymetric for this implies that a counter-meter has supplanted the basic 4-feel. Non-Ewe musicians, however, frequently become re-oriented (disoriented) amidst this complex metric matrix.

Whenever a cross rhythm or displaced meter assumes perceptual dominance, the music appears reconfigured. The perceptual shift makes it difficult to maintain steady tempo and polyrhythmic alignment. Example 4.11, below, is an exercise to help readers master the gakokoe phrase (A: onbeat 4-feel; B: displaced 4-feel; C: onbeat 6-feel; D: upbeat 6-feel; E: 8-beat feel). In each two-staff system the upper staff shows the gakokoe (stems up) and the flow of beats (stems down). The bottom staff is a hand-patting drill; "S" means strong hand, "W" means weak hand, "T" means both hands strike together. I advise readers at first to play both hands on the same surface (thighs, for instance) but, after the physical coordination is mastered, to strike two different surfaces (thigh and desk top) so that the tension in the polyrhythm is highlighted.

Example 4.11
Exercise for learning the polyrhythm of the gakokoe phrase and metric beats.

Swing Feel

Although this musical world of a guiding ostinato (gakokoe phrase) set within a matrix of beats may seem dauntingly complex, well-enculturated Ewe musicals function quite comfortably within it. In fact, they sophisticate the rhythm to an even finer degree through what we might call a swing-style or "elastic" interpretation of the eighth-note pulse. Consider three possibilities for a pair of tones within one 4-feel beat: a straight eighth-quarter interpretation, an even pair of dotted-eighth duplets, or the swing feel. The thirty second-note pulse is needed for precise measurement.

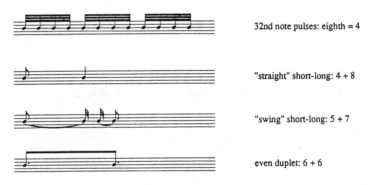

32nd note pulses: eighth = 4

"straight" short-long: 4 + 8

"swing" short-long: 5 + 7

even duplet: 6 + 6

Example 4.12 *Swing style short-long pairs.*

In these materials on Kpegisu the swing pair occurs most frequently in the songs. In drumming the swing feel often surfaces as an anticipation of the eighth note pulse (see the analysis of kagan, below). In Chapters Two and Three the transcriptions do not indicate swing feel. Whenever I write dotted-eighth pairs, in other words, I mean to indicate an intentional foray into a binary interpretation of the 4-beat meter.

Ewe music provides an interesting comparison to the jazz tradition.[5] In jazz, swing eighths are long-short pairs and swing syncopation is after the pulse; here we have the inverse: short-long pairs, and anticipations of the pulse. And just as notation does not fully capture nuances of jazz rhythm, the phenomenon of swing feel makes us realize the limits of explaining timing in Ewe music in terms of precisely regular streams of pulsation. As is true of all musical traditions, notation brings us close but is no substitute for direct sensory experience.

Hand Clapping

Mr. Agbeli does not demonstrate hand clapping (asikpefoḟo) but it is quite prominent in the Wodome video. When members sit and sing, they clap. The most prevalent clapping patterns are 1) the 4-feel beats, 2) the 6-feel beats, 3) the 3-then-2 pattern, and 4) 4-feel beats shaped into the phrase three-four-one (rest on two) (see Example 4.23).

Axatsȩ

In Mr. Agbeli's demonstration all downward strokes on the axatsȩ exactly match strokes on the gakokoe. As this suggests, the rattle and bell work together as a musical team. While the gakokoe supports a great variety of phrase shapes and meters, the axatsȩ confirms the relative importance of several of these interpretations: first, by virtue of its one longer tone the axatsȩ establishes mode 1 as the gakokoe's principal phrase configuration (see Example 4.2), and second, the axatsȩ accents the 6-beat counter-meter, a kinesthetic and sonic fact that can be shown in notation with beams (see Example 4.13). In addition, the axatsȩ helps establish the eighth note pulse as Kpegisu's primary rate of rhythmic motion. The axatsȩ's loud indefinite-pitched sound is vital to the overall energy of the piece.

The Wodome group uses two additional axatsȩ phrases: a) the final stroke (that is, the stroke on beat one) is played on the palm, not the thigh; and b) the stroke sequence in beats three and four is hand-thigh-thigh/-hand-thigh-thigh. In the latter case, palm strokes articulate the 4-feel beats.

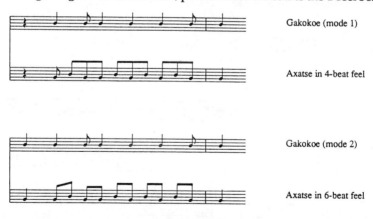

Gakokoe (mode 1)

Axatse in 4-beat feel

Gakokoe (mode 2)

Axatse in 6-beat feel

Example 4.13
Axatse phrase in 4-beat and 6-beat meters.

Kagan

The kagan part centers on brief figures that articulate the second and third partials within each 4-feel beat. This constant offbeating creates powerful polyrhythm. The late Freeman Donkor, one of my teachers at Wesleyan University, often equated the kagan's effect to salt in a stew: it brings out the flavor of the other musical ingredients.

In many repertories of Ewe drumming the kagan player steadily repeats the 2-3-rest figure. Indeed, the kagan players in the Wodome group continuously sound this figure, albeit with swing feel and occasional ornamentation of the second stroke with flams. As demonstrated by Mr. Agbeli, however, the kagan plays variations based on three different two-measure phrases which are spontaneously mixed into an improvised line. These phrases are constructed from three one-measure motives.

What musical effects do I hear in the kagan part? First, it introduces flux and variability into the polyrhythm of the ensemble. Second, it establishes a two-measure frame, although this is not an iron-clad requirement; Mr. Agbeli, for example, does not rigidly maintain the two-measure kagan form. Third, motive A emphasizes the backbeats albeit in a particularly "kagan-

Example 4.14 *Kagan motives and phrases.*

esque," between-the-beats manner. Fourth, because its first pair of strokes hit in unison with bell strokes 3 and 4 kagan suggests a re-configuration of the gakokoe phrase to mode 4 (see Examples 4.15 and 4.2).

Example 4.15
Kagan phrase three and gakokoe phrase starting on stroke 3.

Fifth, kagan accents the two offbeat partials within each 4-beat. Since the lead drum often accents the third partial of beats two and four, kagan often sounds "turned around" (see Example 4.16). Listeners enculturated to the iambic accentuation patterns of Western music (a-1, a-2) are particularly at risk for this type of perceptual disorientation.[6] According to my experience, metric displacement to the second partial of the 4-beat is less prominent.

Cross rhythm works its effects on the kagan part, of course. In the 4-beat perspective, kagan tones always are offbeat but in the 6-beat meter kagan tones are both onbeat and upbeat. In Example 4.17, motives A, B, and C are beamed to the onbeat 6-feel; the upbeat 6-feel is indicated underneath.

As if this were not a sufficiently rich rhythmic situation, Mr. Agbeli is fond of "swinging" the kagan part by playing the first tone in each kagan pair just a bit early. In other words, he anticipates the eighth note pulses and evens out the kagan's short-long triplet quality. When asked to describe the difference between the "straight" and "swing" interpretation of kagan, Mr. Agbeli says the swing style feels faster and more lively. He reports that if the music is dull the kagan player sometimes is told, "*Netso!*" meaning, "It

Third partial accent in onbeat 4-feel

Turned around 4-feel

Example 4.16
Kagan phrase one and turned around 4-beat feel.

Example 4.17 *Kagan motives in 6-beat meters.*

should be faster!" The kagan player is being asked to give his part more push or kick without rushing the tempo or becoming unsteady. These remarks confirm that this effect is recognized by Ewe musicians and not a product of my overzealous analysis! The subtle, lilting swing effect is vital to the Ewe performance style but very difficult for non-Ewes to master. The Wodome video provides excellent study material in this regard.

Kidi

The kidi phrase as presented by Mr. Agbeli may be thought of as two motives, each containing three bounces followed by three presses. As shown in Example 4.19A, the bounces synchronize easily with gakokoe strokes 5 and 6, but create a more challenging polyrhythm toward the beginning of the bell phrase. The Wodome group uses a different kidi phrase in their fast drumming: four presses and two bounces, the bounces coming on the second and third partials of beats two and four (see Example 4.19B). This phrase closely resembles kagan motive A in Mr. Agbeli's style.

Kidi's evenly-spaced tones seem to prove empirically the existence of the eighth note pulse. However, Mr. Agbeli gives the part a subtle rubato

Example 4.18 *Swing feel in kagan phrase three.*

Example 4.19 *Kidi phrases and the gakokoe part.*

flavor by slight delaying the second tone within each 3-stroke. I often experience "beat turnaround" when he demonstrates the swing-feel kidi; that is, I hear the second partial within each 4-beat as an onbeat moment (see Examples 2.6 and 4.20B). In the fundamental 4-beat meter the third tone within each three-stroke figure is onbeat, but the kidi phrase sounds different when the metric orientation shifts. In Example 4.20 the 4- and 6-feel beats appear above the kidi phrase which is beamed to indicate the metric gestalt.

Ewe drummers conceive the kidi part to be in a musical dialogue with the lead drum. This conversational framework is most apparent when the lead drum themes neatly interlock with kidi. In Example 4.21 the lead drum's bounces anticipate the "kidigi" phrase while the presses mark the start of kidi's open tones.

The Ensemble Polyrhythm

The polyrhythm of the drum ensemble appears in Example 4.22 below; the first measure of each staff shows a phrase's beginning and the second

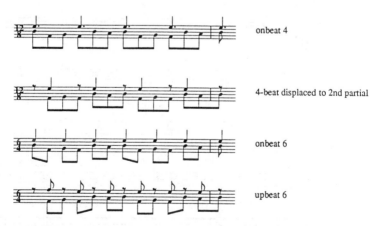

Example 4.20 *Kidi phrase in 4- and 6-beat meters.*

Example 4.21
Conversational relationship between kidi and lead drum.

measure indicates repeated play. Each voice is distinctive in its own right, yet has powerful impact upon the others. An instrument's part is multifaceted; its manifold qualities only emerge as its phrases repeat over-and-over. The phrases weave in and out of each other to make an integrated texture. The ensemble's music is a deep and dynamic world of sound in time.

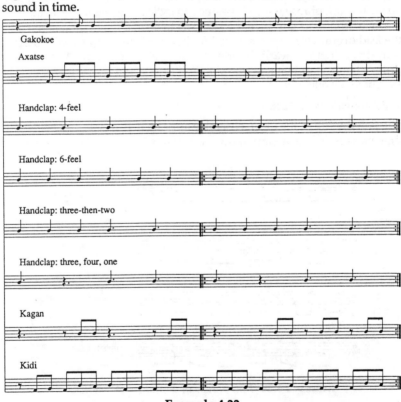

Example 4.22
Polyrhythm of gakokoe, handclaps, axatse, kagan, and kidi.

Chapter Five

The Lead Drum

Within the polyrhythm of the drum ensemble and amidst the dancing, singing, and dramatic display of the performance, lead drummers create variations on traditional themes using characteristic techniques of improvisation.

This chapter synthesizes both theoretical and practical perspectives on the music of the lead drum. I endeavor to describe the style and content of Mr. Agbeli's lead drumming and also help folks learn how to do it themselves. First, the principal themes from Mr. Agbeli's demonstrations are analyzed according to their internal structure as well as their fit within the polyrhythm. Next are presented the improvisational procedures by which Mr. Agbeli spins these themes into variations. Finally, the variations themselves are arranged in a taxonomy (a hierarchical chart). I propose a model of improvisation and suggest that this framework meaningfully corresponds to the musical process of the lead drummer.

Lead drumming is never random. Its resources include 1) remembered and invented "licks"; 2) appropriate techniques of improvisation; 3) characteristic kinesthetic patterns of hand movement; 4) polyphonic cross-talk with the other instruments; and 5) inspiration from songs and dancers.

In this book the lead drum's music is systematically presented for detailed study in three different ways. First, in Chapter Two we can follow Mr. Agbeli's musical thinking in an uninterrupted performance context. Second, the analyses of themes and variational procedures in the body of this chapter identify the music's principal fixed elements and dynamic forces. Third, the taxonomy of variations at the chapter's end not only permits the study of phrases one-by-one but also demonstrates improvisational techniques in action. By chaining variations together readers can create stylistically appropriate improvisations. Readers will be greatly assisted by referring to the audio/video programs. Words, charts, and notation are no substitute for seeing and hearing African experts in action.

Before embarking on this rather technical enterprise, let us consider the lead drummer's range of responsibilities in performance.

The Role of the Lead Drummer

The lead drummer co-directs the performance. The order and duration of sections in the performance is determined by an informal consensus among lead drummer, song leader, and elders. Elders (*vumegawo*; big men for drumming) sitting outside the dance circle gauge the pacing of the event. If the group seems bored they may suggest a change in tempo to the drummer and lead singer; if the members' enthusiasm wanes they may call for a round of drinks. The lead drummer also has input into the flow of the performance and has the prerogative to extend or shorten a performance segment. Just as song leaders prefer the Songs Interlude section, drummers like the introductory Adzo when they are alone "in the limelight." Mr. Agbeli uses the image of fingers on the hand to explain relationships of authority among the leaders of the performance: they are utterly interconnected.

An effective lead drummer must communicate with the dancers. As mentioned in Chapter One, Kpegisu is danced in short bursts of movement: people rise in small groups, dance side-by-side across the dance ring and back, and then return to the benches. The drum-dance connection in Kpegisu is flexible, especially in comparison with other more flamboyant Ewe dances such as *Adzogbo* in which every lead drum phrase is precisely linked to a specific dance figure. Two features of the lead drummer's communication with dancers seem especially significant. First, his depth of musical understanding, creativity, and inner feeling should put everyone in the mood to dance. An event can go on despite weak singing, but if the drumming is shabby a performance can never be a success. Second, he should loosely align the sections in his improvisation with the dance. When people are up and ready to dance, it shows respect if the lead drummer acknowledges them with a new passage of improvisation. Sometimes he may cue them to begin with a special phrase (see theme A, below) but since the dance ring is usually quite busy, this is not a hard-and-fast rule.

The lead drummer studies individual dancers. A dancer may signal the drummer to begin a new series of variations by raising his arms, a gesture that means, "I am dancing." In the videotaped performance of the Wodome Kpegisu group several dancers gave this salute during the Adzo. It is especially sweet if the drummer plays a dancer's drinking nickname (*ahanonko*) or other pet rhythm.

As the featured percussionist in the drum ensemble, the lead drummer controls the momentum of a performance. Always exciting, the music should patiently gather intensity. For example, when Mr. Agbeli reaches a musical peak in his lead drum demonstrations he plays a phrase (see theme C, below) which interrupts his chain of ideas, thereby suspending the music's flow and permitting a re-ignition of its energy. Mr. Agbeli says that an ideal performance starts well, grows beautifully, and ends nicely.

Musical Form

For "Kpegisu to be Kpegisu," so to speak, a distinctive set of themes must be played on the lead drum. Although we may distinguish their differences, most lead drum themes are quite similar to each other. In fact, the part is so homogeneous in character that Mr. Agbeli says the lead drummer develops his music from only one rhythm. This is clearly demonstrated in his performance of lead drumming using mnemonic syllables (see Example 2.11). In his view, all the themes—those of the grandfathers and those from today—are traditional. After all, he argues, dead musicians created the old rhythms in much the same fashion today's drummers invent new ones. It is likely that in the olden days the lead drum literally spoke, but I suspect that most contemporary Ewe players think of these phrases as absolute music, not as a form of surrogate speech.[1] Mr. Agbeli, for instance, reports that he does not know drum language for Kpegisu.

The drummer is expected not only to present Kpegisu's themes virtually intact but to develop chains of related variations using improvisational procedures that also are typical of Kpegisu. By exploring the dynamic potency of the themes, he often generates new ideas which themselves may become the basis for subsequent passages. Thus, the musical form of Kpegisu's lead drum part can be seen as a series of episodes improvised from preset and original thematic material. Kpegisu's episodic form is subtle. Perhaps because it need not be linked dramatically to the dance, the lead drum frequently shifts between themes without fanfare. Although he sometimes brackets thematically coherent passages with special drum riffs, Mr. Agbeli often moves seamlessly between episodes. The extent to which a phrase functions as the seed of a set of related variations is an important consideration in my identification of discrete episodes within his flow of ideas.

Formal relationships among successive episodes are characterized by either a) repetition; b) sequence; or c) juxtaposition. Since drummers fashion their improvisations from just a few seminal ideas, it is not surprising that they frequently return to the same themes. In my view, this type of repetition is best characterized as an exploration of musical depth rather than a lack of imagination. Sometimes a new episode organically develops from its predecessor. As Mr. Agbeli works with one idea, another related concept catches his fancy and becomes the germinal seed of a new series of phrases. He reports that in improvisational Drums such as Kpegisu he does not know what ideas will come to his mind, what music his body will produce. Prepared in technique and conception, experienced but retaining an open mind, he waits for fresh ideas to spark forth from the traditional material.[2]

As discussed in Chapter Four, the ever-repeating "support" parts in the drum ensemble create a dynamic equilibrium. The lead drum part, on the other hand, has a more linear movement through time. Themes have characteristic effects, virtual personalities, which the drummer juxtaposes for dramatic contrast. Qualities which distinguish one theme from another include: 1) polyrhythm with the gakokoe phrase; 2) phrase length; 3) accentuation pattern; and 4) internal design, that is, the density, timbre and timing of strokes. For example, themes 1 and 8 present very different musical personae (see Example 5.2): theme 1 begins on gakokoe stroke 7, covers two beats, and accents the upbeat 6-feel cross rhythm; theme 8 moves from beat three to cadence on beat one, is two gakokoe cycles in duration, accents the 4-beat, and features rapid three-stroke rolls. In my own performance experience, I have noticed that theme 1 deepens the music, sending players and listeners into a virtual polymetric trance; theme 8, on the other hand, zips along with zest derived from its tight interlock with kagan.

It is fascinating to realize that the idea that some phrases are stronger or more complex than others is foreign to Mr. Agbeli's musical sensibility. While recognizing that cross rhythm and syncopation might make a phrase more difficult for a non-Ewe musician to play, he states that these factors have no bearing for him: "Drumming is like talking, you simply bring the words out." On the other hand, he does differentiate phrases which fit easily with the gakokoe from those which are "out from the bell," and when playing with newcomers he carefully chooses his rhythms so as not to throw people off. I suspect that Ewe players are fully aware of the musical and affective qualities of the phrases with which they craft their improvisations.

Themes

Having sketched the scene of the drummer in performance context and discussed the part in general terms, we turn to a detailed consideration of the lead drum phrases. I begin with thematic ideas found in Mr. Agbeli's demonstrations. In the musical examples below, repeat marks mean "repeat ad libitum"; where necessary the *al segno* sign indicates the beginning of a phrase. The gakokoe part always is provided as reference. Please refer to Ex-

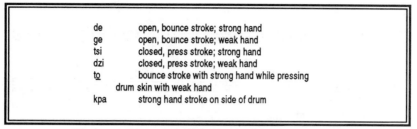

de	open, bounce stroke; strong hand
ge	open, bounce stroke; weak hand
tsi	closed, press stroke; strong hand
dzi	closed, press stroke; weak hand
t̜o	bounce stroke with strong hand while pressing drum skin with weak hand
kpa	strong hand stroke on side of drum

Chart 5.1 *Mnemonic syllables for lead drum strokes.*

ample 2.1 for a key to the notation of drum stick strokes; mnemonic syllables are shown in Chart 5.1).

Signal Themes

Four themes always are presented whole, as is, and never become seeds for passages of variations (see Example 5.1).[3] Mr. Agbeli says these riffs give his playing a distinct design. I call them "signals" because they are linked to dance and the drummer's control of the performance.

Theme A ends an episode and alerts dancers that a new episode soon will begin. Mr. Agbeli uses this phrase to mark the end of a passage of creatively enchained variations and to return to the main Kpegisu theme (see theme 1, below). It is his means of "wiping the slate clean," so to speak, before beginning another sequence of variations.

The phrase usually is announced with an accented weak-hand press stroke on beat four which cuts off the preceding passage of improvisation. Perhaps because it conveys essential information, theme A has a very distinctive design of three brief motives: motive 1 begins on the second partial of beat one and moves press-bounce-bounce-press on the eighth note pulse to the second partial of beat two; motive 2 moves bounce-press-bounce-press from beat three to beat four; motive 3 lies on the upbeat 6-feel cross rhythm and can be heard either as the third part of theme A or as the beginning of the next improvised episode. I particularly enjoy hearing theme A as the sum of two separate rhythms—the press strokes of the weak hand and the bounce strokes of the strong hand.

Theme B simply is a three-stroke roll repeated ad libitum at the discretion of the lead drummer. This theme calls to the dancers, alerting them that the drummer is embarking upon a new passage. Frequently, Mr. Agbeli uses a four-part sequence: he a) ends an episode with theme A; b) moves briefly

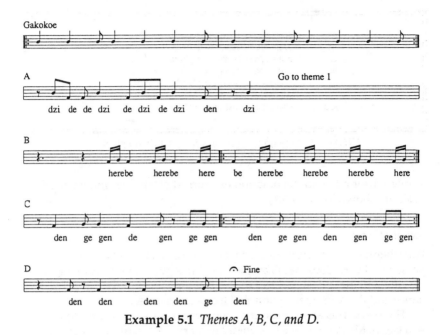

Example 5.1 *Themes A, B, C, and D.*

to theme 1; c) calls the dancers with theme B; and then d) launches into a new passage.

Theme C occurs only at strategic points in these "solos." Although to my ear the phrase arrests the music's flow with a wonderful polyrhythm against the gakokoe, Mr. Agbeli does not hear it as "out from the bell." Since in his choreography this phrase brings dancers out to center stage, we can say that like theme B this phrase functions as a holding pattern which precedes an episode for the dance. Notice, by the way, the similarity between the relationship of gakokoe strokes 2-4 to beat two and theme C's three weak-hand strokes which surround beat four; imitation of this kind is characteristic in Ewe drumming and singing.

Theme D is the ending signal. Aligned with mode 2 of the gakokoe phrase (see Example 4.2), all its tones occur in unison with the gakokoe. The omission of bell stroke 4 from the drum phrase, however, highlights the way the bell part switches from offbeats (strokes 1-2) to onbeats (beats four and one).

Seminal Themes

Musically, themes A-D stand apart from other themes because they are fixed musical objects. Much more typically, themes are worked and re-worked into chains of connected variations. This process balances what can be termed static elements and dynamic processes: by static elements I mean the brief ideas that are repeated and modified within improvised passages; dynamic processes are the procedures for shaping these themes into varia-tions—lengthening, shortening, embellishing, and so forth. I will discuss the seminal ideas here and their musical "children" in the section on im-provisation below.

I have distilled Mr. Agbeli's lead drum demonstrations into a set of eight principal themes (see Example 5.2). Given its importance in the design of the part, the "den dzi" idea is called theme 1. The other ideas are arranged to reveal their musical affinities. Themes 1 and 2 both consist of two strokes timed to the upbeat 6-feel cross rhythm but they lie in different places within the gakokoe phrase. Themes 3 and 4 also are almost identical—both contain three strokes with a bounce-press-bounce sequence of timbres that accents the 4-feel, but theme 3 moves "4 a 1" in synchrony with gakokoe strokes 6-7-1, while theme 4 moves "1 y 2," setting up a more contrasting polyrhythm. Themes 5 and 6 are alike save for the timbre of their first two strokes, but I have separated them because they inspire quite distinctive variations. In theme 7, Mr. Agbeli doubles the kidi phrase with his presses and develops his episodes by adding bounces before and after this brief fig-ure. Finally, theme 8 is a trademark two-measure phrase in Mr. Agbeli's Kpegisu style.

This inventory is made for the purpose of clarifying Mr. Agbeli's musical thought and action. The analysis is tactical; I do not assert its validity as eth-nographic fact for the Ewe musician and realize that it may overstate the number of discrete themes. Themes 1, 3, 4, and 8 project strong identities and I feel comfortable asserting their musical integrity, but whether the other themes deserve such status is more questionable. Theme 2, for ex-ample, could be heard as a variant of theme 3; themes 5, 6, and 7 very jus-tifiably could be conceived as variants of theme 1. On the other hand, given the number of variants within each category (see Example 5.5), one could argue for a larger list of themes.

In my view, the relationship between the lead drum and the other per-cussion parts is reciprocal. Each theme projects its musical identity yet simultaneously is shaped by its setting within the sounded and implicit facets of Kpegisu's music. Seminal ideas have charisma, so to speak, but

Example 5.2
Eight principal lead drum themes.

also draw power from the musical energy fused into the gakokoe and other parts in the drum ensemble. Because the spontaneous episodes which they catalyze are shaped by the musical personalities of these lead drum themes, it is good to explore them in more detail before digging into the subject of improvisation.

Improvisation

At the outset of this section, a word of caution: this explicit, technical approach to music differs radically from the education in the oral tradition of a traditional Ewe drummer like Mr. Agbeli. Through direct exposure to drumming and rote imitation of other musicians, he learned his art in an un-

---

Theme 1: Puts maximal pressure on the standard 4-beat meter and normal phrasing configurations; talks easily with kidi; feels smooth and tends to slow the rate of rhythmic movement; creates "turn around" onto the upbeat 6-feel or displacement of 4-feel to the third partial; always used after theme A as a bridge to theme B but also as a theme on its own; very important theme.
• *Internal Structure:* two beat duration; 6-beat pace; sparse, smooth texture; bounce-press timbre; silence on beats two and four.
• *Gakokoe:* start on stroke 7; unisons with strokes 4 and 5.
• *Meter and Cross Rhythm*
4-beat: places strong accent on third partial of beats two and four, and weaker accent on second partial of beats one and three.
6-beat: strongly accents upbeat of beats six, one, three, and four.
Cross rhythm: 3:2 with 4-beat; moves 2 3 1 toward implicit cadence with 4-beat on beats two and four.
• *Within Ensemble*
Gakokoe and axatse̱: reinforces configuration starting on stroke 7; maximal gestalt switch.
Kaga̱n: unison of open tones with second stroke creates "turn around" effect.
Kidi: press stroke marks beginning of bounce-stroke figures.

Theme 2: Closely resembles themes 1 and 3; pushes the 4-feel but has more offbeat effect than theme 3 because the cadence on beats one and three is omitted; synchrony with gakokoe within beat four, polyrhythm within beat two.
• *Internal Structure:* two beat duration; 6-beat pace, but feels "in four;" sparse, smooth texture; bounce-press timbre; silence on beats one and three.
• *Gakokoe:* start on stroke 6; unisons with strokes 6, 7, 4.
• *Meter and Cross Rhythm*
4-beat: accents the onbeats and third partials of beats four and two.
6-beat: feels "in four" despite alignment with beats five, six, two, and three of the upbeat 6-feel meter.
Cross-rhythm: 3:2 with 4-beat, moves 1 2 away from moment of simultaneity.

Chart 5.2
Musical qualities of lead drum seminal themes.

• *Within Ensemble*
Gakokoe and axatsę: reinforces characteristic movement.
Kagan: open tones anticipate, closed tones accent second stroke.
Kidi: overlaps with final open tone.

Theme 3: Strongly aligns with all other parts; firm 4-beat accentuation; synchrony with gakokoe in beats four and one, polyrhythm in beats two and three; its effects are the virtual opposite of theme 1; very important theme.
• *Internal Structure:* two beat duration; 4-beat pace; medium density, smooth shape; bounce-press-bounce timbre; no silence.
• *Gakokoe:* start on stroke 6; unisons with strokes 6, 7, 1.
• *Meter and Cross Rhythm*
4-beat: powerful movement four-one, two-three.
• *Within Ensemble*
Gakokoe and axatsę: reinforces fundamental meter and phrasing configuration.
Kagan: tightly interlocks.
Kidi: clear interlock.

Theme 4: Despite its many similarities with theme 3, creates more intense polyrhythm because of short first stroke; establishes polyrhythm within beats one and two and a more synchronous feeling in beats three and four; very similar to themes 5 and 6; effectively drives the time and intensifies the mood; used as principal theme in the fast drumming section of the Wodome Kpegisu group.
• *Internal Structure:* two beat duration; 4-beat pace; busy and intense/jagged texture; bounce-press-bounce timbre; no silence.
• *Gakokoe:* start on stroke 1; unisons with strokes 5 and 6.
• *Meter and Cross Rhythm*
4-beat: powerful movement one-two, three-four; accentuation on second partial of beats one and three.
• *Within Ensemble*
Gakokoe and axatsę: reinforces configuration beginning on beat one.
Kagan: interlocks and anticipates.
Kidi: overlaps the open tones and thus interrupts rather than converses.

Theme 5: Seems designed with kidi in mind; normally strongly 4-beat in orientation with clear accentuation of beats one and three but if second stroke is omitted, becomes identical with theme 1.
• *Internal Structure:* two beat duration; 4-beat pace, but with hint of 3:2; busy, but smooth texture; timbre moves from bounce to press; silence on beats two and four.
• *Gakokoe:* starts on stroke 7; unisons with strokes 7, 1, 4, and 5.
• *Meter and Cross Rhythm*
4-beat: strong accentuation on onbeat and second partials of beats one and three.
6-beat: if onbeat bounce is omitted accentuation shifts to the upbeat 6-feel.
Cross Rhythm: sounds the 3:2 relationship (quarter:dotted-quarter) except for the moment of simultaneity.
• *Within Ensemble*
Gakokoe and axatsę: reinforces configuration starting on stroke 7.
Kagan: follows rather than anticipates.
Kidi: clear conversational relationship.

Chart 5.2, continued.

Theme 6: While a virtual clone of theme 5 it is used as the basis for longer, more sparsely textured phrases; anticipates and overlaps with kidi; uses only press strokes so allows the ensemble to move into prominence. See themes 5 and 1 for discussion.

Theme 7: Incorporates kidi and lead drum parts into one line; within passages of improvisation draws upon ideas from themes 1 and 5; like theme 6 uses only press strokes so is quiet and in the background. See themes 5 and 1 for discussion.

Theme 8: A distinctive and very important traditional theme; noteworthy features include two-measure phrase length, loud mute strokes, three-stroke rolling figures, and beat-by-beat "a-3, a-4, a-1" movement; engages kagan in very intense interlock but feels expansive because of its longer duration.
• *Internal Structure:* two measure duration; 4-beat pace; very busy texture; one measure of bounces, one measure of muted "to" strokes; silence on beat two.
• *Gakokoe:* starts on stroke 4; unisons on strokes 6, 7, and 1.
• *Meter and Cross Rhythm*
4-beat: powerful three-four-one movement; moves from pickup to onbeat.
• *Within Ensemble*
Gakokoe and axatse: reinforces fundamental configurations.
Kagan: very intense interlock.
Kidi: clear dialogue within beat one, but overlaps completely within beat three.

Chart 5.2, continued.

mediated, multi-sensory, non-literate manner. Far from focusing on the technical aspects of Kpegisu's music, he is more concerned with ethics than aesthetics, with cultural values, performance dynamics, and the projection of his personality.[4] Nevertheless, I go boldly into analysis.[5] In my opinion, the model of improvisation presented below adequately represents Mr. Agbeli's performance style and sometimes I even assert that he thinks this way musically, if not verbally. But we must be careful not to "let the tail wag the dog." His performance stands whole and complete. It is not "merely" the enactment of abstract concepts which have a higher value or more privileged status.

My approach serves a significant, yet limited, goal: helping the cultural outsider to understand Kpegisu as a musical art. First, I point out the impact of playing technique upon musical thinking and action. Second, I discuss the processes Mr. Agbeli uses to build thematically coherent episodes. Third, I present an inventory of the variations on each thematic type found in these demonstrations. In conclusion, I present my views on the overall musical qualities of the lead drum part.

Playing Technique

Not only an intellectual, emotional, and sonic experience, Kpegisu is a kinesthetic act as well.[6] The lead drum part entrains the musician in comfortable and familiar patterns of movement which bear directly on rhythmic design. These motions are a ready aspect of technique; drummers know their musical potential and the effects they project. The drum, Africans say, plays itself: the musician is a conduit through which tradition passes.[7]

Consider the musical consequences of the apparently unremarkable observation that drummers play with one stick in each hand: if they strike steadily on the eighth note pulse each stick will hit on every other pulse thus automatically creating 3:2 with the tacit 4-feel beats (see Example 5.3). Furthermore, because each hand creates its own steady flow, both the onbeat and upbeat 6-feel meters are materialized. We see that the 3:2 patterns so important to the rhythm of Kpegisu are rooted in the body.

Among the instruments of Kpegisu, only kidi alternates hands in this steady manner. Three timing sequences are particularly important in the lead drum part (see Example 5.4): a) on the quarter note pulse; b) in a form of 3:2; and c) on the third and first partials of the 4-feel beats (a-3, a-4, a-1). Two stroking patterns on the quarter note pulse seem most prevalent: strong-weak-strong (5.4.A1), and strong-weak-weak (5.4.A2). The first is used in theme 1 variations; the second in themes 3 through 7. By adding a strong hand stroke between the two weak hand strokes, the drummer easily transforms the second pattern into 3:2 played strong-weak-strong-weak (5.4.B). Finally, the strong hand often strikes on the third and first partials of 4-feel beats (5.4.C). This pattern is found very clearly in themes 8 and B.

These patterns of movement are the physical component of the improvisatory process on lead drum. (In Example 5.4 "S" indicates strong hand, "W" indicates weak hand.)

Eighth note pulse; stems down: weak hand; stems up: strong hand

Weak hand: onbeat 6-feel   Strong hand: upbeat 6-feel

Example 5.3 *The kinesthetic setting of 3:2.*

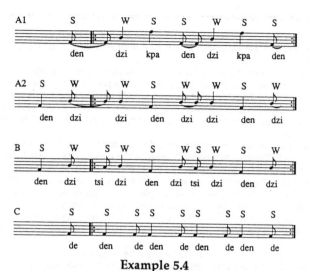

Example 5.4

Characteristic patterns of hand movement in the lead drum part.

Improvisational Procedures

For the purposes of this analysis we assume that the lead drummer is thoroughly at home with all the many elements of Kpegisu discussed in this book: the performance context, the dance, the gakokoe phrase, the matrix of pulses and beats, the ensemble polyrhythm, the songs, and the preset lead drum themes. Now we turn our focus to the construction of lead drum "solos" within the framework of these resources and constraints. I begin simply by describing a segment of Mr. Agbeli's lead drumming (see Chart 5.3). I have chosen Example 2.10 because it demonstrates the interaction between lead drum and kidi.

This performance segment illustrates how Mr. Agbeli builds chains of related phrases by applying stylistically appropriate variational procedures to Kpegisu's themes. The following list summarizes the dynamic devices I find in his lead drumming demonstrations (see Chart 5.4).[8]

I propose a model of improvisation with three components: a) dynamic forces, that is processes for musical modification; b) static elements, that is, themes; and c) flux elements, that is, variations. A acts on B to produce C.[9] My point about the nature of lead drumming is this: we can understand Mr. Agbeli's playing as an application of these instruments of musical modification to the traditional themes of Kpegisu.

- Measures 1-6: Gakokoe and kidi get started. Mr. Agbeli enters with theme C; this phrase, which never is the seed idea of a passage, appears again in measure 99 as a means of suspending the discursive flow of ideas.
- Measures 7-10: The improvisation starts with an heraldic drum roll, "herebegedege den gi." In mm. 8-10 Mr. Agbeli plays very sparsely, using "kpa" strokes and presses to highlight the upbeat 6-feel and "talk" to the kidi. These thematically neutral phrases could be classified within themes 1, 2, 5, or 6.
- Measures 11-14: Without any transition phrase, he changes to theme 3. In measure 13 he uses a short connecting roll moving toward beat four to transform the two beat theme into a flowing one-measure phrase.
- Measures 15-19: This is the standard sequence of cuing dancers and marking musical form: theme A, theme 1, theme B. The figure "herebegidegi" in measure 17 precedes and leads up to the theme 1 seed idea. It is similar to the flourish in measure 7 but placed differently within the gakokoe phrase.
- Measures 19-27: The drum roll merges with theme 8. After just two repetitions (mm. 19-22) Mr. Agbeli replaces the drum roll "herebe herebe herebede" (mm. 21-22) with a motive that rhymes with the "to" strokes, "den toto, den toto." The whole variation, which lasts two measures, is cleanly divided into a motive four beats in duration, "toto toto toto," followed by two motives of two beats each, "den toto, den toto." All elements in the variation are directional, that is, they push toward cadence on beats three or one.
- Measures 28-32: Again, Mr. Agbeli marks the form in the standard way.
- Measures 32-42: The next episode begins with the seed idea of theme 6. In his first variation Mr. Agbeli leaves out tones (m.33), thereby accenting the third partial of beats two and four. Then he adds tones on beats three and one (mm.35-36) to create intense interlock with kidi. His next sequence toys with phrase length: lengthening it to two measures with a bounce-stroke fill on beat four (mm.37-38), shortening this to a one-measure form (m.39), and finally reducing it to a two-beat length (m.40). The similarity of this variation to the seed idea of theme 3 seems to induce him to make a seamless transition to a new series of variations that I classify as a separate episode (mm.42-47).

Chart 5.3.
Description of lead drum demonstration, Example 2.10.

In my view the pertinent question to ask of this schema for improvisation is not abstract, subjective, and mentalistic: Does this model truthfully represent how Mr. Agbeli conceives and executes his music? Certainly, Mr. Agbeli does not talk in these terms. "I try to think of things to play that make the music sweet," is his description of improvisation. "We just do it, we do not talk about it," is a favored response to technical questions. But this is not surprising. Like artists everywhere, Mr. Agbeli experiences music nonverbally as a holistic integration of technique, structure, meaning, effect . . . I am more interested in the objective, pragmatic question: Does this model yield relevant musical insight in an elegant manner?[10] Or simply: Does it help us hear the music?

In chart 5.5 below, I use this model of improvisation to interpret from start to finish another of Mr. Agbeli's lead drum "solos" (see Example 2.8).

1) Repetition: repeating a musical thought.
2) Segmentation: isolating and repeating a shorter motive from within a longer phrase.
3) Connection: joining shorter motives into a longer phrase by filling in musical silence.
4) Culmination: preceding a short motive with a lead-in figure.
5) Idea substitution: maintaining the rhythmic character of a phrase, but changing one of the figures within it.
6) Stroke substitution: changing stroke type without changing timing.
7) Syncopation: playing a tone at a delayed or anticipated moment.
8) Ornamentation: using grace-notes or brief rolling figures.
9) Omission: silence; leaving out an expected tone.

Chart 5.4 *Improvisational features in lead drumming.*

Within this demonstration I hear nine distinct passages (A-I), a passage consisting of a set of variations arising from one theme.

This chart demonstrates how the model of improvisation provides a language for analysis that yields relevant insight into this musical tradition: column two shows the static elements (seminal themes); the comments in column four highlight the dynamic processes listed in Chart 5.4; column three reveals the constant inventiveness and subtle manipulations at play in Mr. Agbeli's drumming. It seems to me that this analysis proves the utility of the proposed model but readers must evaluate for themselves. Certainly as I have said over-and-over in these pages, no analysis can replace the value of non-verbal, non-literate musical study.

Note: Column 1 indicates the measure in which the phrase begins; repeat markings do not affect measure numbering. Column 2 is the theme classified according to the set of eight seminal ideas discussed above; variations are numbered in the order they appear in this "solo"; for example, the marking "2c2" means: second theme type, third variation, second subtle distinction (such as stroke substitution or embellishment). Column 3 shows the number of times played; this statistic reveals the rate of change in his playing. Column 4 contains comments.

Passage A

4	Ca1	3	First stroke played earlier than written.
5	Cb1	1	Press stroke substituted for first bounce stroke.
6	Ca1	4	Normal stroking resumed.

Passage B

7	2a1	1	Theme 2 introduced with a flourish.
8	2b1	4	Seed idea clearly stated.
9	2a1	1	First variation repeated.
10	2c1	1	Two-measure phrase built by isolating and repeating the drum roll figure from 2a1; final stroke in roll changed to a bounce.

Chart 5.5
Themes and variations in lead drum demonstration, Example 2.8.

12	2c2	1	Same variation repeated but with final stroke changed to a press.
14	2a	2	Return to a one-measure flourish with slight changes in timing and timbre.
15	2b1	2	Seed idea clearly stated.
16	2d1	1	One-measure variation created by filling in the rests between restatements of the seed idea.
16	2e1	1	Two-measure variation built by isolating and repeating the fill used in 2d1.
18	2b1	2	Seed idea restated.
19	2e2	1	Restatement of two-measure theme with bounce strokes substituting for press strokes in fills.
21	2d2	1	Restatement of one-measure variation using press strokes.
22	2b1	4	Seed idea restated.
23	2a1	2	Opening variation restated.
24	2b1	2	Seed idea restated.

Passage C

25	B	na	Rolling figure announces a new episode.
27	8a1	4	Seed idea stated.
29	8b1	3	Variation by isolating and varying the "to̱" stroke figure from the seed idea.
33	8c1	3	One-measure phrase using only the "to̱" stroke figure.
34	3a1	4	Abrupt change to another theme with no transition. This theme not developed into an episode.

Passage D

36	A	1	The dance-cue, form-marker phrase.
37	1a1	3	Seed idea stated.
38	1b1	1	Seed idea extended to one-measure span by anticipating and filling in with a characteristic drum roll flourish.
41	1c1	9	One-measure idea shortened by isolating and repeating the roll.
44	1a1	5	Seed idea restated.

Passage E

45	6a1	2	Abrupt switch to a new seed idea. In this demonstration theme 6 appears only in this two-measure form.
49	6b1	5	Two-measure phrase shortened to two beats by isolating and repeating its final figure.
51	6c1	3	One-measure variation created by using silence in beat two.

Passage F

52	A	1	Standard use of the dance-cue signal.
52	1a1	1	Since it is played only once, the "den dzi" which straddles mm.52-53 seems to be an integral part on dance-cue signal.
53	B	na	The "roll call" completes this characteristic combination.
55	4a1	1	Seed idea stated.
55	4b1	1	Two-measure variation made by leading into the fourth appearance of the seed idea with a fill on the pickup to beat one.
57	4c1	2	Two-beat variation made by isolating and repeating the fill figure.
58	4b1	1	Mr. Agbeli returns to the two-measure variation.
62	4c1	4	Again he follows with the two-beat variation.
63	4a1	4	Seed idea stated; the press stroke timed to bell stroke 7 marks the end of the episode and prepares for signal A.

Chart 5.5, *continued.*

Passage G		
65 A	1	Form-marker phrase clearly closes the episode. .
65 1a1	2	Standard use of theme 1 to bridge between the dance signalling themes A and B.
67 B	na	"Roll call" completes the classic form.
68 8a1	3	Seed idea clearly stated.
72 8b1	3	Standard theme 8 variation.
Passage H		
75 A	1	Form-marker phrase clearly closes the episode.
75 1a1	5	Rather than bridging to theme B, theme 1 used as the basis for an episode.
77 1d1	2	One-measure variation made by filling within beat four.
77 1e1	1	In the repeat Mr. Agbeli builds a two-measure variation by isolating and repeating the fill figure.
79 1d1	2	Return to the one-measure variation.
79 1e2	1	In the repeat the two-measure variation reappears with only bounce strokes in the fills.
81 1a1	2	Seed idea restated.
Passage I		
82 8d1	2	One-measure phrase that could have been classified as a theme in its own right but also can be conceived as a variant of the "to̲" figure from theme 8.
83 8e1	2	In the repeat the phrase length is expanded to two measures with a powerful rolling figure reminiscent of passage B.
86 8b2	2	Standard theme 8 variation using press strokes rather than "to̲" strokes.
88 8d2	1	One-measure variation made by isolating the "to̲" stroke figure of theme 8 using press strokes.
89 E	1	Ending signal.

Chart 5.5, *continued.*

Inventory of Variations

Mr. Agbeli does not improvise by mechanistically combining pre-established phrases.[11] On the contrary, he makes spontaneous decisions in response to all aspects of Kpegisu's music as well as the performance situation. Nevertheless, he does improvise in a characteristic style using ready sequences of variations. The final step in this breakdown of the lead drum part, therefore, is a taxonomy of the themes and variations in Mr. Agbeli's performances (see Examples 5.5-5.12). The variations are arranged according to the improvisatory techniques listed above (see Chart 5.4). For example, 1.1 is the seed idea of theme type 1, variation 1.2 is made with ornamentation, variation 1.3 by connection within beat four, 1.4 and 1.5 by segmentation and repetition, 1.6 by idea substitution and culmination, and so forth. The inventory, in other words, has a pragmatic educational use: it teaches how chains of variations grow from seed themes.

Overall Musical Qualities

Analysis dissects music. Engrossed in its details, we miss the whole. Perhaps it is good, therefore, to conclude this chapter by answering several deceptively simple questions about lead drumming in Kpegisu.

What are its salient rhythmic characteristics? First, the part has a march-like drive, especially in the themes which accentuate the 4-beat meter and use the trademark three-stroke roll. This four-square effect, I hasten to add, takes place within a very swinging, polyrhythmic setting. Second, in contrast to this steady 4-feel onbeating, there are three principal patterns of off-beat and/or cross rhythmic accentuation: 1) on beats two and four; 2) on the upbeat 6-feel cross rhythm; and 3) on the third partial of beats two and four.

What guides the lead drummer's specific musical decisions? Musical form is linked loosely to the dance. Within the episodes of enchained variations, improvisation is influenced by all elements in Kpegisu's percussion music: 1) the matrix of pulses and beats; 2) the gakokoe phrase; 3) the ensemble parts, especially the conversation with kidi; and 4) the lead drum themes. Variations are generated according to normal procedures of Ewe drumming style as well as by typical kinesthetic patterns. Songs and the drama of the performance also effect his playing.

In a more general sense, what are the musical goals of a drummer like Mr. Agbeli? I posed this question to him. Interestingly, the metaphor of "telling a story on the drum" did not seem right to him. He simply tries to play something that will make the music sweet. He said that he wants to get a vibration, to experience a thrilling feeling.[12] He also mentioned his desire to give respect to his ancestors by playing in the style of the old people.

I would emphasize three other goals. First, he intensifies and deepens the musical moment through a) repetition; b) subtle change; and c) striking contrast.[13] Second, he projects his spirit and charisma toward other members of the drum ensemble, the dancers, the singers, and onlookers. The power of his personality is magnified by a generalized sense of ethnic pride, and a feeling of participation in the Kpegisu heritage.

Finally, at risk of sounding trite, we could say that Mr. Agbeli's drumming affirms life. Kpegisu is a war music—life and death were its original subjects and even now its songs evoke images of suffering in a hard world. Mr. Agbeli's playing conveys an aura of aggressiveness that, for me, borders on violence. His clean, hard blows seem to strike like an executioner's axe. Yet in a wonderful paradox, as these "killing" blows vibrate the drum skin, their sound broadcasts a message of life.

Inventory of lead drum themes and variations
Example 5.5
Theme 1 variations.

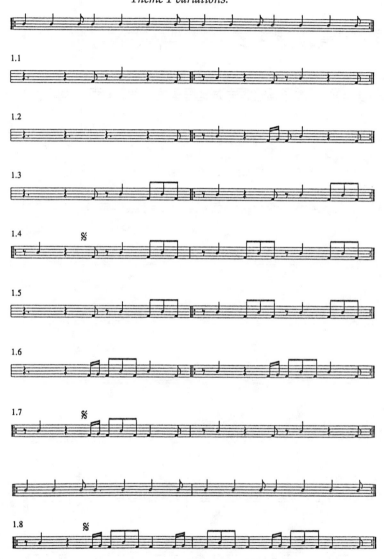

Example 5.6
Theme 2 variations.

Example 5.7
Theme 3 variations.

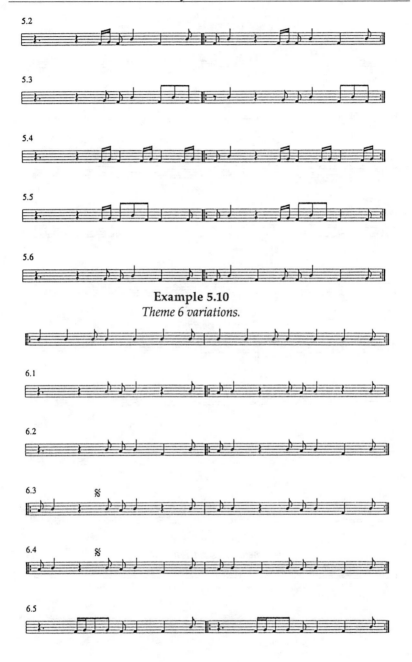

Example 5.10
Theme 6 variations.

Example 5.11
Theme 7 variations.

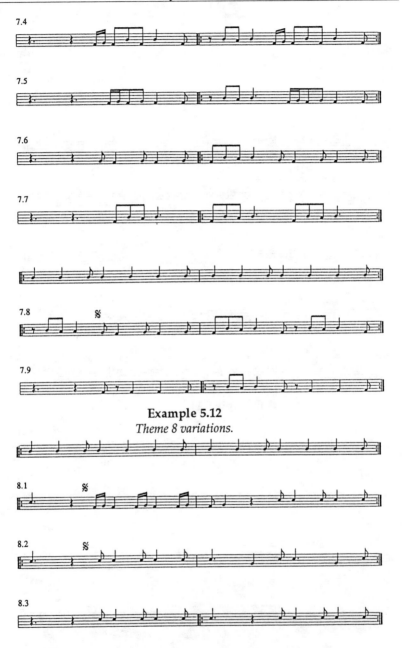

Example 5.12
Theme 8 variations.

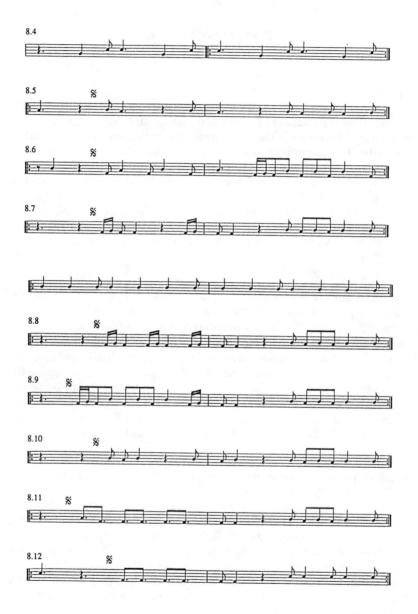

Chapter Six

The Songs

*T*his chapter presents analysis of Kpegisu songs. After a definition of terms, I discuss a handful of exemplary songs and then, with "music in our ears," I summarize the characteristics of text and music found in the collection as a whole.

Throughout the chapter I concentrate on the connection between a song's text and the musical elements of form, tonality, melody, and rhythm.[1] My challenge is to show how the experience of meaning derives, in large measure, from the synthesis of language and music.[2] In this way the analysis of music becomes relevant to the interpretation of culture.[3]

Definition of Terms

My discussion of the musical structure of these songs uses a technical vocabulary that certainly is *outside* the local Ewe vernacular, but, as is true throughout this work, I believe that the musical experiences to which these terms refer are *inside* the Ewe perspective.[4] Without a doubt, however, this enterprise of detailed theoretical analysis is foreign to a traditional Ewe sensibility. Since the discussion is complex and lengthy, at the outset I define the concepts and terminology used in my analysis.[5] Although many terms undoubtedly are well known to most readers, it seems to me that cross-cultural communication is optimized when the meaning of the analytical lexicon is clear. Key terms appear in bold type face.

Basic Elements: Pitch, Interval

In performance, **pitch** is experienced as a tone's position (highness or lowness) within a melody; in analysis, its relative location within a pitch set or mode is paramount. A pitch and its octave duplications are a **pitch class**. All pitches in a song are its **pitch set**. In my musical notation, pitch is **relative;** songs have been transposed to facilitate comparison of melodic and modal structures. **Intonation** means the precise pitch of a sung tone. Because I will regard variation in intonation as a *stylistic* rather than *structural* feature of this music (see *Tuning,* below), a song's pitch set and its pitch classes are rather small finite sets.[6] **Interval** refers to the difference in pitch between two sung tones. Three categories of interval are prominent in analysis: **major (M), minor (m),** and **perfect (P).**

Tuning

I will not engage in much discussion of what we might call the **tuning system** of Ewe song. Although I hear distinctive Ewe patterns of intonation, my analysis accepts that the relative pitch of a sung tone can be designated *with reasonable accuracy* using the widely known system of twelve **semitones** (m2) to the octave.[7] As listeners to the Kpegisu taped programs surely will hear, however, the pitches and intervals as performed ofen differ from those as written. This discrepancy I attribute to stylistic norms of intonation rather than intentional and consistent use of musical structures such as **neutral intervals** (between minor and major) **equidistant pentatonic scales** (the octave divided into five equal intervals), and so forth. In one significant case, F in the hemitonic scale, a pitch is identified as being variable intoned within a **pitch band** tather than sung on an intended **pitch point** located precisely among the twelve semitones within the octave. Sound comes first—notation represents it; readers should refer to the audio cassette in order to know exactly how pitches are intoned. I neither assert that these songs operate in accordance with the laws of acoustics nor that my analysis is "The way they hear it," but I do believe that an important dimension of Ewe song is identified from this point of view: the interplay between tonality, melody, and the musical expression of ideas and feeling.

Scale, Tonality, Mode, Modulation

A song's pitch classes arranged in ascending/descending order constitute a **scale.** According to my analysis, these songs employ **pentatonic** scales (five pitch classes per octave) of two types: **hemitonic** (with m2) and **anhemitonic** (without m2). A song's pitch set may have more than five pitch classes, however, because of **added pitches** (pitches used only in certain melodic/tonal contexts). A scale is called a **mode** when information about tonal/melodic function is introduced.[8] Pitch classes in modes and scales may be called **degrees** and designated with Roman numerals I-II-III-IV-V-VI-VII-VIII.[9] Degrees may be **sharpened** (raised) or **flattened** (lowered) by a minor second. I shall use **tonality** as an inclusive term referring to the organization of pitch including pitch set and scale type, relationships among modal degrees, and patterns of melodic movement.

A mode has a **tonic,** that is, the pitch class of melodic resolution, the tone towards which melodies move, the tonal center. Frequently, the tonic is the

finalis, that is, the final tone in a phrase. When I say, "The phrase is in E," I mean E is its tonal center. Other pitch classes within the mode acquire their melodic function in relation to the tonic. I will refer to a pitch's quality of melodic/tonal attraction as its **tonicity,** and the melodic process conferring tonicity to a pitch as **tonicization;** a pitch which temporarily functions as a tonal center has been **tonicized.** The tonic is degree I in its mode. In these songs tonicity is felt not simply as a pull towards I, but as a tonal **affinity** between pitches separated by a P4 or P5. **Cadence** means melodic movement towards and arrival on a given pitch, often, but not always, the tonal center. A **closed cadence,** movement to the tonic, feels **resolved;** on the other hand, an **open cadence,** movement to a non-tonic pitch, is **unresolved** and not in melodic/tonal stasis. Although I distinguish between resolved and unresolved melodic feelings, the dichotomy between **dissonance** and **consonance** does not seem to be relevant in these songs.

Over the course of an entire song there is a **progression** of tonicized pitches within one mode and, in some songs, **modulation,** that is, a change in tonic pitch, the establishment of a new tonal center. What differentiates modulation from tonicization? First, tonicization is rather brief, but modulation is in effect for a longer duration and has a stronger impact on melody; second, modulation may involve the introduction of new pitch classes; and third, modulation is more significantly connected to sectional form. During the process of modulation, a portion of the melody may function as a **pivot,** that is, it simultaneously fits within the pre-existing and newly established tonal centers.

Melodic Structure and Bi-tonicity

A **melody** is a succession of tones sung in musical time (pitch fused with rhythm). A song consists of melodic **phrases,** each roughly equivalent to a line of poetic text. Successive phrases often establish **antecedent-consequent** relationships. A phrase often consists of shorter units which I shall term **subphrases.** Melodies employ **steps** (M2, m2) and **leaps** (M3, m3, P4, P5, m6) in three types of melodic movement: 1) **stepwise,** 2) **step-leap** or **leap-step,** and 3) **leap-leap. Contour** describes melodic direction (descending, ascending, undulating). The span of a song's pitch set is its **range.** In these songs melodic phrases often occur within segments of the pitch set which I shall term the lower, middle, and upper portions of the range. The range of a specific melodic phrase is its **tessitura.** Melodic phrases and/or cells often occur within the range of a **trichord** (interval of M3 or m3), **tetrachord** (interval of P4) or a **pentachord** (interval of P5). Successive tetra-

and pentachords are termed **conjunct** when they overlap, and **disjunct** when separated by a scale step.

Significantly for melodic and tonal structure in these songs, a m7 range is created by conjunct tetrachords (I-IV, IV-VIIb); on the other hand, an octave range is formed by conjunct tetra- and pentachords (I-IV, IV-VIII) and disjunct tetrachords (I-IV, V-VIII). **Melodic sequence** (the repeat of a phrase at a different tessitura) occurs abundantly in conjunct and disjunct tetra- and pentachords. This means that phrases within adjacent tetra- and pentachords frequently tonicize degrees I, II, IV, V, and/or VIIb. As a consequence, many songs feel **bi-tonal,** that is, several modal degrees compete for tonicity and the song has an unresolved quality.

Form

Performers experience **sections** within the songs as an interplay of 1) text, 2) call-and-response arrangement among Leader, Group, and All (Leader and Group together), and 3) musical structure. A **rounded** form, ABA, is most characteristic: A, an opening call/response, is followed by B, a contrasting call/response, and then All **reprise** the A section. Typically, the first two sections are repeated (AABBA), and frequently, All sing a new section of text before the reprise (AABBCA). A few songs have **linear** form (A1 A2 A3 A4, or A1A1 B1B2), but, as will be discussed, even these achieve a feeling of musical return through modulation.

Arabic numbers indicate significant melodic/tonal variation between repeated sections; for example, the marking A1A1 B1B2 C1 A2 accommodates the following: A1A1, the opening call/response is repeated exactly; B1B2, there is a modulation in the repeat of B; C1, a third section is sung once; A2, in the reprise only the Group response is sung. In this book I do not designate phrase structure within a section; for example, an opening section that contains several phrases in both the Leader and Group parts still is labelled A.

Modulation usually occurs at junctures in a song's form. Because they link together the opening and closing A sections, the B or C sections function as **bridge passages.** In a song's progression of tonicities, modulation within the B2 or C1 sections functions as a **turnaround** that propels the melody into the reprise.

Texture, Improvisation, and Harmony

The **texture** of these songs is a function of two factors: the number of people singing at once and the presence of **melodic variation** and **harmony.** Clearly, this musical attribute is directly affected by call/response arrangements:

the part sung by the song leader and his assistants (Leader) has fewer voices than the parts sung by the other performers (Group) or all the singers together (All). In other words, the Leader part has what we might call a lighter weight and thinner texture than the other two parts. In these materials Kpegisu songs are presented as **monophonic** (one voice), but this is misleading. In fact, Ewe singers have a very keen **polyphonic** sensibility as displayed in the Wodome-Akatsi video program. Although my discussion is limited to **horizontal** factors, a complete picture of these songs must include analysis of their **vertical** (the **sonority** of simultaneous tones) dimensions, as well.[10] This is an important caveat to these materials on Kpegisu songs since improvised melodic variations and harmony are among their essential attributes.

Rhythm

Songs are rhythmic compositions. Each song has its own rhythmic design determined by the duration and order of its tones and silences, the plan of its phrases, its relationship to the bell phrase, and its fit within the meter(s). Sometimes a song's rhythm is in **unison** with portions of the bell phrase or the beats; at other times it may create an independent **contrapuntal** line that contrasts polyrhythmically with the other parts. We may distinguish between **onbeat** and **offbeat** or **syncopated** tones. In the ensuing analysis the one onbeat and two offbeat moments within a dotted-quarter note beat in the 4-feel meter are indicated with numbers (1 2 3). The vocables "ta" and "ti" will indicate **long** and **short** tones (quarter and eighth notes). Two- or three-note units are called **rhythmic elements**. A **pickup** is a short offbeat tone that precedes on onbeat tone. Two-note ti ta elements timed 1 2 (3) characteristically are performed as **swing eighths.**

Accent means rhythmic emphasis. In discussions of cross rhythm when I say "The rhythm accents a 3:2 cross rhythm (upbeat 6:4-beat, quarter:dotted-quarter) phrased two three one," I am referring to a phrase that begins on the second of three implicit quarter note beats, proceeds through the third beat, and ends on the first beat, that is, the moment of simultaneity between the two beat systems. Rhythms of this type often are sounded out with four tones, ti ti ta ta, the first being a pickup, the second and fourth being onbeats. This is the **resultant rhythm** or **horizontal** form of 3:2 (quarter:dotted-quarter).

The fundamental rhythmic setting for the songs is established by the bell phrase and the 4-feel beats and it is for this reason that the transcriptions in Chapter 3 are beamed strictly to the dotted-quarter beats. However, beaming to the 4-feel beat visually obscures what might be called a song's surface "lilt." The analysis below presents alternate transcriptions which clarify my interpretation of the rhythmic setting of the text. These are challenging rhythms. The scores might best be deciphered in stages: first, clap the text rhythm and then try to chant the words while clapping; second, tap your foot to the 4-beats while clapping and/or speaking the text rhythm; finally, foot tap the 4-beat, hand clap the bell phrase, and speak the text.

Text

Songs may be regarded as poems set to music. Most songs carry a didactic implication, that is, they teach right ways of living. *More than the purely musical factors outlined above, it is the meaning of the text that is of central concern to Ewe performers.* Each song addresses one or more themes such as destiny, death, ethics, history, war, public image, group relations, ancestors, money, family life, and/or suffering. Themes may be expressed directly, but more often are alluded to indirectly by means of proverbs and various figures of speech. A variety of poetic devices are used such as discontinuity in theme, time or voice, and rhyme. Clever word play, in other words, makes an important contribution to a song's effect. In addition to these semantic considerations, the sonic aspects of language also have an impact upon music. In particular, melody is affected by speech tone since *Eʋegbe* (the Ewe language) is a tonal language with three levels of spoken intonation which are notated as follows: low \; mid -; high /; rise-fall ^.[11]

Characteristic Songs

Throughout this book, I endeavor to keep performed music "at center stage," so to speak. Analysis serves the music, the music does not demonstrate the analysis. At this point, therefore, I will introduce significant patterns of text, scale, form, melody, and rhythm (numbered ❶ through ❺, respectively) by discussing specific songs. Only after whole songs are considered will I move on to summary and conclusion(❻).[12] I will begin with slow-paced songs (*Ʋu Blewu*), then unmeasured (*Ayoḏeḏe*) and fast-paced (*Ʋutsotsoe*) songs. Because analysis may seem to dismember songs into lifeless elements, let me restate my goal: to show how culturally-grounded meaning arises from the interplay of language (song text) and music.

Ʋu Blewu Songs (Slow pace)

The first three songs *Gbe Yi Gbe Me Ku La*, *Xe No Ha Mee Me Nye*, and *Mie Ku Ano Lo*, are chosen because they represent the three principal scale/mode types used in this collection: 1) anhemitonic pentatonic scale with E as tonic,

2) anhemitonic pentatonic scale with D as tonic, and 3) hemitonic pentatonic with B as tonic.

GBE YI GBE ME KU LA (Song 4, slow pace, anhemitonic, E mode)

❶ *Text*

Let us consider first the meaning of the words. The song's ostensible subject is what Mr. Agbeli calls a "bad death," that is, an untimely death perhaps caused by an automobile accident, a sudden physical injury, or a childhood disease. In such cases, the burial must be made in the night and without certain rites; for example, the head will not be shaved and the hair and nails will not be saved for a second burial and honorific memorial service. The lack of a public funeral makes it plain that such a death is unwanted; the spirit of the deceased will not reincarnate and continue the misfortune within the family. The poem conveys the emotional impact of a bad death. The first line hooks us at once—who has not contemplated the day of their death—and then *Kɔsi*, an Ewe everyman, speaks for us all; we empathize with his plea not to be buried in the night, with his head partly shaved, left alone for the townspeople to observe and his family to be disgraced. The image of *Sakpate* killing children with smallpox is poignant and chillingly unsentimental. Mr. Agbeli explains that the villagers know Sakpate, the deity associated with smallpox, as enforcer of ethical standards and traditional customs. The song, therefore, imparts an implicit didactic message: live a proper moral life and avoid this miserable fate.

L:	Gbe yi gbe me ku la	1
	Kɔsi be miga kɔm ade zayu ne mia di o	2
G:	Dakpo na nɔ ta nama.	3
	Ye dilawo mi ga nlom be de o he	4
	Du nku na kpɔ mia wo o. {2x}	5
L:	Sakpate wo ku ame wum he.	6
G	:Deviwo kua wɔ nublanuia. {2x}	7
A:	Gbe yi gbe me ku la	8
	Kɔsi be miga kɔm ade zayu ne mia di o	9
	Dakpo na nɔ ta nama.	10
	Ye dilawo mi ga nlom be de o he	11
	Du nku na kpɔ mia wo o.	12

L: The day that I die
      Kọsi says, "Don't carry me into a night lorry to bury
G: My head to remain partly shaved.
      My buryers, don't forget me alone
      For the town's eye to look at us." {2x}
L: The smallpox death is killing people.
G: Children's death is miserable. {2x}
A: The day that I die
      Kọsi says, "Don't carry me into a night lorry to bury
      My head to remain partly shaved.
      My buryers, don't forget me alone
      For the town's eye to look at us."

Now let us see how the music conveys the meaning of the text.

❷ *Pitch Set and Scale*

The melody's range and pitch set are shown in Example 6.1. The scale is an-hemitonic pentatonic; B and F♯ are added pitches used only in descending stepwise movement to g and d1. Melodic phrases are set primarily within trichords and conjunct tetrachords; one pentachord occurs at a strategic location—the B section.

❸ *Form*

The song text has a rounded form, AABBA. The comparatively long A section (lines 1-5) about Kọsi's fear of a pitiful death is sung twice in call-and-response format: the Leader sets the scene and introduces Kọsi; the Group follows the thread of Kọsi's plea to its conclusion. The shorter B section (lines 6-7) about children dying of smallpox also is repeated; after the Leader states that people are dying, the Group focuses the image on children. Singing together, Leader and Group reprise the opening call-and-response (lines 8-12). In performance, the entire song is repeated approximately four times.

When both text and melody are taken into consideration, the song's form is seen as A1A1 B1B2 A1. The tune can be parsed into ten short melodic subphrases (see Example 6.2). The Leader's opening phrase is built with three subphrases (1-3) which tonicize the main pitches in the song: D, A, and E. The Group responds with two melodic phrases (subphrases 4-7). The first phrase (subphrases 4, 5) returns the tonicity to D; the second phrase (subphrase 6, 7) retraces the Leader's descent A, E. Since these phrases are identical in the repeat, I label this section A1A1.

Now, the bridge passage. Leader's phrase contains two subphrases (8-9). The first time through the poem the Leader's phrase tonicizes the A-E axis. I count the Group's response as subphrase 10; it tonicizes E. When the text is sung the second time the Leader (subphrases 8 and 9') tonicizes D, not E as before. The Group (subphrase 10') also confers tonicity to D. Given the change in melody, I label the B section B1B2. Finally, All repeat the whole A section.

❹ *Melody, Mode, and Tonality*

The song's tune moves between Dᵇ and E tonicities: D-E-G-A-C (I-II-IV-V-VIIᵇ) and E-G-A-C-D (I-IIIᵇ-IV-VIᵇ-VIIᵇ). Section A1 begins in D and ends in E. The three subphrases in the Leader's part are all in D; the finalis on E (II/D) feels unresolved. The Group begins in D—subphrases 4 and 5 resolve the Leader's open cadence (E-D)—but then modulates to E via interlocking descending P4 movement, c1-g, a-e. The modal pivot is c1-g in mm.4-5 (VIIᵇ-IV in D, VIᵇ-IIIᵇ in E). Section B1 retains E as tonal center: the Leader boldly leaps to the upper tonic (a-e1, subphrase 8); the Group (subphrase 10) extends and confirms the descent to the lower tonic (a-g-e) found in the Leader's second subphrase (subphrase 9). In Section B2, however, the tune returns the tonic to D: after repeating the a-e1 leap, the Leader descends

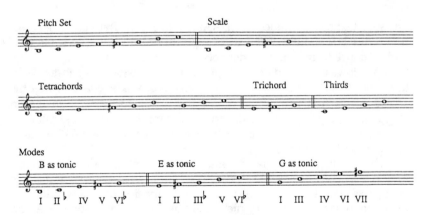

Example 6.1
Pitch materials in Gbe Yi Gbe Me Ku La (anhemitonic pentatonic, E mode).

only to d1 (subphrase 9'); the Group confirms the new tonal center (subphrase 10'). The reprise of section A1 continues the D feeling but ends in E.

The contour of the melody contributes to the song's sense of tonal progression and forward movement. In A1, the Leader begins at the top of the range and then undulates downward to the lowest pitch. In its response, the Group reaches toward the upper tetrachord but then stays at mid level before ending on e. The same progression of tessituras is repeated in B1, but at a quicker rate. In B2, however, the melody remains in the upper range, adding to the power of the E-D modulation.

In general, melodic ascent/descent conforms to the contour of the text's speech tones, but it is important to recognize that there are plenty of excep-

Example 6.2 *Melodic phrases in Gbe Yi Gbe Me Ku La.*

tions and this factor does not override the "logic" of the melodic/tonal design.[13]

L: Gbè yī gbè mē kú lá
      Kǫsí bē mìgà kǫ̀m ā- dē zàvú né mìā ḏiò
G: Ḏàkpō nà nǫ̀ tā námà
      Yè ḏìláwó mì gà̱n-lòm bē dì ò hè
      Dù̱n-kú ná kpǫ́ mīa wó ò
L: Sākpātē wó kúà- mè wūm hè
G: Ḏèvíwó kūà wǫ̀ nùblánúia

Melodic/tonal action is linked to sectional form and call/response relationships. Section A is bi- tonal: with A acting as a mediating pitch (V of D, IV of E), it moves from D to E but doesn't really settle on either. Section B1 clearly is in E; section B2 firmly moves to D and functions as a turn-around into the reprise of the bi-tonal A section. Antecedent phrases have ascending melodic movement and high tessitura which create musical excitement and intensity; consequent phrases have melodic descent within the mid to low range. With regard to melodic movement and tonal progression, the Group's role is to confirm and/or resolve the Leader's tonality and bring the melody to rest in the lower end of the range. When the Group departs from this norm by raising the tessitura in subphrase 10′, the sense of turnaround is intensified.

❺ *Rhythm*

In section A, the Leader's phrase divides into two rhythmic units, subphrase 1 and subphrase 2-3 (see Example 6.3). Subphrase 1 suggests a quarter-note triplet: it is phrased two three one, begins on the pickup to beat four and cadences on beat one. Subphrases 2-3 make a phrase of six beats characterized by three eighth-quarter (3-1) pairs followed, as if in climax, with an eighth-eighth- quarter element. The Group response has two phrases. The first (subphrases 4 and 5) is built with three two-note elements: subphrase 4 suggests 3:4 polymeter (phrased three one two), while the syncopated placement of the quarters in subphrase 5 contrasts with the onbeat tones of subphrase 4. The second phrase (subphrases 6 and 7) neatly balances three-, two- and one-note elements within a mirror form (3 2 1 2 3). In terms of the all-important fit with the gakokoe part, we see that vocal rhythm exists in counterpoint with the bell. The rhythm in section B tends toward unison with the gakokoe. In the Leader's phrase, subphrase 8

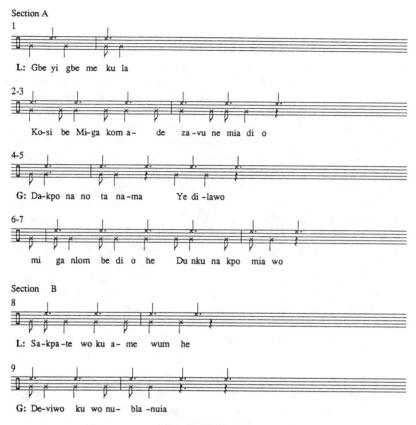

Example 6.3
Rhythmic phrases in Gbe Yi Gbe Me Ku La.

horizontally manifests the 3:2 cross rhythm between upbeat 6- and 4-feel beats. The Group response (subphrase 9) begins right on beat three but then switches to the upbeat 6. Although the pitches change in B2, the rhythm stays the same. Summing up, in section A the song introduces an independent rhythmic line into the music's overall polyrhythmic texture; on the other hand, in section B the song rhythm is timed according to the gakokoe and the implicit beats of the polymetric matrix. In both sections crucial words in the text are set on the rhythmically prominent first beat: *ku*, death (m.2), *zaʋu*, night lorry (m.3), *ta*, head (m.4), *wum*, killing (m.8).

❺ *Conclusion*

Isolated in analysis, these musical ingredients are experienced holistically in performance. The theme of the poem is death. Its two subjects are divided between the two major sections of the form: A—a bad death, and B—death from smallpox. In A Leader and Group share the story, in B they juxtapose related but discontinuous remarks. Musical distinctions between the two sections frame the change in subject. The A section is musically more complex: the range and pitch set are larger, the rhythm is contrapuntal, the phrases are longer, the melody is more active, and it is bi-tonal. In B the music is more starkly bold: the melody has wide leaps, the tonic modulates from E to D, and the rhythm flows with the bell and beat matrix. Throughout the song musical elements focus attention on important words and phrases; for example, in the Group response in B2 the modulation to D dramatically highlights the image of children's death.

The music not only is intended to serve the text, however. It offers its own inherent satisfaction. Consider the contrast and balance between A and B sections: whereas the sophisticated A section repeats exactly, the simple B section contains a turnaround, that is, the E to D modulation. The complementary interaction of its musical elements create a sense of surprise and resolution, ordered progression, and drive to the song.

XE NO HA MEE ME NYE (Song 9, slow pace, anhemitonic, D mode)

❶ *Text*

This song praises the generous, community-spirited person and recommends membership in drum and dance mutual aid societies. Bird imagery conveys this message. The singers, like birds in a flock, gain advantages from their group and boast that sickness will never kill them. The solitary hawk envies this more social way of living. A man named Nake, perhaps the composer himself or the person to whom the song is dedicated, refers to himself as an only child who is treated as a brother by the townspeople, presumably because of his cooperative behavior.

L:	Xe no ha mee me nye he.		1
	Ye wo be nye me ku na do wo ku o he.		2
G:	Xe no ha mee me nye he.		3
	Ye wo be nye me ku na do wo ku o. {2x}		4
L:	Papayesue gblom be,		5
G:	Gbosusua nu nyuie adee. {2x}		6

A: Nake gblɔm be nye ḏeka koe danye dzia.   7
Nye ḏeka koe nye duawo nɔvi.   8
Be naneke ya me wɔm o.   9
Xe nɔ ha mee me nye he.   10
Ye wo be nye me ku na dɔ wo ku o.   11

L: I am a bird inside a group.
And they say I will never die from sickness.
G: I am a bird inside a group.
And they say I will never die from sickness. {2x}
L: Hawk is saying that
G: To be many is a good thing. {2x}
A: Nake is saying that I am the only issue of my mother.
I am the only brother of the townspeople.
So nothing happens to me.
I am a bird inside a group.
And they say I will never die from sickness.

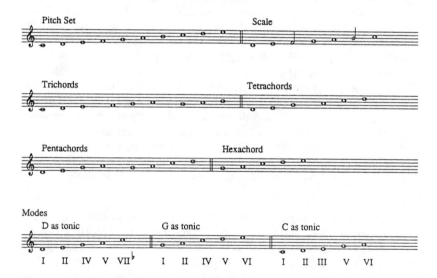

Example 6.4
Pitch materials in Xe No Ha Mee Me Nye (anhemitonic pentatonic, D mode).

❷ Pitch Set and Scale

The range is from c to e1 (see Example 6.4). The pitch set includes c-d-e-f-g-a-b-c1-d1-e1. Like *Gbe Yi Gbe Me Ku La*, the scale is anhemitonic pentatonic; F and B are added pitches introduced to permit stepwise movement around the tonicized pitches G and A respectively. Melodic phrases occur within trichords (c-e, f-a, g-b), tetrachords (d-g, a-d1), and pentachords (d-a, g-d1). Penta- and trichord frequently combine into a hexachordal frame, for example, g-e1 as a sum of g-d1 and c1-e1.

❸ Form

The song text has the extended rounded form, AABCA. In the A section (lines 1-4), Leader and Group sing the same text, albeit with different melodies. This echo-like call/response is repeated. The poetic text is shared in the B section (lines 5-6): the Leader introduces the hawk's voice and then the Group tells us what is on his mind. This section also is repeated but with a change in melody, as we will see. The C section (lines 7-9), sung together by Leader and Group, is about Nake. Finally, All reprise the two lines of the A section (lines 10-11).

The melody elaborates the poem's form thus, A1 A1 B1 B2 C1 A2 (see Example 6.5). The four lines of text in A section are rendered in two melodic phrases, each with two subphrases. The Leader's part (subphrases 1 and 2) is in G; the Group (subphrases 3 and 4) tonicizes D. The two lines of text in the B section are sung in two phrases; the first time through both Leader and Group (phrases 5,6) tonicize D, but in the repetition the tonicity shifts m7 upward to C. Given this modulation, I label B section B1B2. Line 7 in section C becomes a long, modulating melodic phrase that I divide into two subphrases: subphrase 7 is in C, but subphrase 8 moves to D. Text lines 8 and 9 are sung in one phrase whose two halves (subphrases 9 and 10) tonicize first C, then D. Only the Group part is sung in the reprise of the A section. This phrase confirms D as the song's primary tonal center.

❹ Melody, Mode, and Tonality

Although it has the same scale as *Gbe Yi Gbe Me Ku La*, this song's tune moves between D, G, and C tonicities: D-E-G-A-C (I-II-IV-V-VII♭), G-A-C-D-E (I-II-IV-V-VI), and C-D-E-G-A (I-II- III-V-VI). Section A1 presents the song's tonal resources: the Leader's opening phrase (subphrases 1,2) hints at tonicity for D and C and establishes G as the mediating pitch between conjunct tetrachords d-g, g-c1; the Group begins on c1 and d1 (subphrases 3,4), but them drops to the lower range and firmly tonicizes d with two

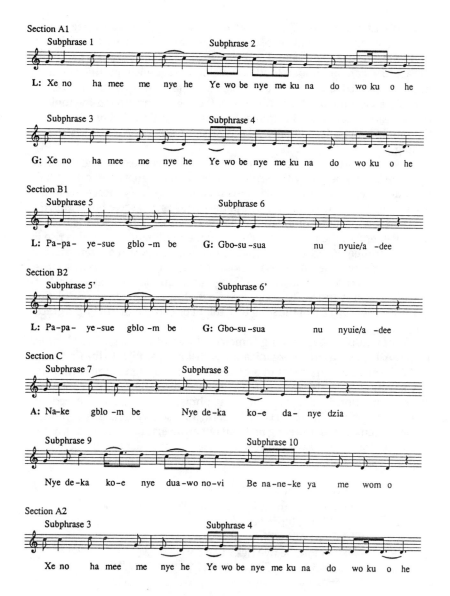

Example 6.5
Melodic phrases in Xe No Ha Mee Me Nye.

types of cadence, g-e-d (IV-II-I) and c-e-d (VII♭ -II-I). The Leader begins section B1 (subphrase 5) with an ascending P5 leap and cadence to a (felt as V of d); the Group cadences to d (subphrase 6). In B2 the Leader's part (subphrase 5') can be understood as melodic sequence in the conjunct pentachord g-d1 that causes the tonal center to shift upward to c1. Once again, the Group (subphrase 6') fulfills the role of confirming the tonicity of the Leader's phrase. The four subphrases in section C play with the D-G-C tonic ambiguity. Finally, the reprise of section A reasserts the D feeling.

Tessitura and contour contribute to the song's sense of musical drama. In A, the Leader begins with ascent into the song's highest range, then falls to mid-range; the Group, too, begins high but its phrase descends to the lowest pitch. In B1 we find the same pattern of ascent-descent but within the mid and low portions of the range; B2, on the other hand, ascends back to the upper end of the range. Together with the modulation to c1, this rise in tessitura imbues B2 with a strong sense of musical forward movement. The C section draws upon all these melodic and tonal elements. In this sense, each of its two phrases extends, prolongs, and summarizes the musical action of sections A and B. The song closes in the low range with an undulating descent which, in light of the song text, might be compared to a bird's graceful landing.

Although this second song tonicizes different pitches (D-G-C rather than E-A-D), its pattern of organization is strikingly similar to the first song: section A uses long phrases in a gradually descending contour and is bitonal; section B has shorter phrases in an ascending contour and contains a clear modulation. Throughout the song phrases are linked in antecedent-consequent pairs. Like *Gbe Yi Gbe Me Ku La*, this melody generally conforms to the speech tones of the song text, but not always; for example, look at the Group resonse in B1. Ewe musicians, it seems, may suspend the semantic impact of speech tone within the specialized context of song.

L/G: Xè nọ̀ hà mée mē nyē hè
       Yè wó bē nyè mé kū nā dọ̀ wó kú ò hè
L: Pápāyèsùé gblọm bē
G: Gbọ̀sūsùa nú nyúie á- dée
A: Nákē gblọm bē nyè dèká kòé dànyê dzìa
       Nyè dèká kòé nyē dùawó nọ̄vī
       Bé nánéké yá mé wọ̀m ò

❺ *Rhythm*

Since they sing the same text, it is not surprising that Leader and Group have the same rhythm in section A (see Example 6.6). I enjoy hearing the two phrases in section A as a rhythmic rhyme. Each subphrase begins with two pickup-to-onbeat figures (ti ta), but the antecedent phrases (subphrases 1 and 3) articulate beat one (ti ti ta, *me nye he*) while the consequent phrases (subphrases 2 and 4) do not (ta ta, *do/wo ku/o*). In section B the Leader takes up the rhythm of the consequent subphrases; the Group responds with the horizontal 3:2 cross-rhythm, "ti ti ta." Section C begins and ends with familiar rhythmic material (subphrases 7-8, and 10), but subphrase 9 is different because it pushes through beats one and two with short-long pairs. Here, the turnaround toward the reprise is accomplished rhythmically.

❻ *Conclusion*

Once again, it is worth emphasizing that music and text are indivisible in performance. Yes, music does help convey the poetic meaning; for example, the resolving musical quality of the Group part in section A has the semantic effect of confirming/affirming the meaning of the words; on the other hand,

Section A
1-4

Xe no   ha mee   me   nye he   Ye wo be nye me ku na   do   wo ku o

Section B
5-6

Pa-pa-   ye-sue   gblom   be   Gbo-su -sua   nu   nyuie a-de

Section C
7-8

Na-ke   gblom   be   nye de -ka   koe   da- nye dzia

9-10

Nye de -ka   koe   nye   duawo no-vi   Be na-ne-ke ya   me   wom o

Example 6.6 *Rhythmic phrases in Xe No Ha Mee Me Nye.*

the musical excitement of the modulation in the Group part in B2 and the rhythmic turnaround in subphrase 9 emphasize the text's message at those points. But, the sheer beauty of the melody plays an important role in developing the song's affective power.

MIE KU ANO LO (Song 8, slow pace, hemitonic, B mode)

❶ *Text*

Like *Xe No Ha Mee Me Nye*, this song is about social life and generosity but instead of focusing on the positive, the composer complains that his family is greedy. His relatives fail to recognize that in helping him, they benefit themselves as well: "The townchild is the one who builds the town." Evidently, his family has a long history of selfishness. Warming to his plight, the songsmith violates the custom against speaking ill of the dead and accuses his ancestors of stinginess. "Look at the dead ones for me. The living ones are also coming," that is, "This is how my forefathers acted and now their descendants are doing it too!"

L:	Mie ku ano lo. Devie nye de.	1
G:	Fonyemeawo de be mie ku ano lo. Devie nye de. {2x}	2
L:	Mikpo kukuawo nam da lo.	3
G:	Gbagbeawo ha gbona. {2x}	4
A:	Fonyemeawo de awo num alea be nku nye adze	
	tsieawo dzi. {2x}	5
	Mie ku ano lo. Devie nye de.	6
	Fonyemeawo de be mie ku ano lo. Devie nye de.	7

L: You are greedy. The townchild is the one who
     builds the town.

 G: My family, I say, "You are greedy. The townchild is the
     one who builds the town." {2x}

L: Look at the dead ones for me.

G: The living ones are also coming. {2x}

 A: My family has done this to me and I remember the dead. {2x}
     You are greedy. The townchild is the one who builds the
     town.
      My family, I say, "You are greedy. The townchild is
     the one who builds the town."

❷ *Pitch Set and Scale*

This song uses dramatically different pitch material than the two songs discussed above: it has semitones (see Example 6.7). The range is B-c1, the pitch set is B-c-e-[f♯ area]-g-b-c1, the scale is hemitonic pentatonic. As mentioned in my remarks on tuning, the F is variably intoned in Mr. Agbeli's performance: 1) F♯, 2) F♮, or 3) in-between the sharpened and natural forms. In most melodic contexts the F pitch class does not require precise intonation—anything within the F pitch band will and does suffice—but in one phrase the sharpened and natural forms are contrasted for melodic/tonal purpose. Melodic phrases primarily occur within tetrachords (B-e, f♯-b, g-c) and the e-g trichord. Melodic movement in major and minor thirds (c-e-g-b) also is important.

❸ *Form*

New scale notwithstanding, the song uses the familiar extended rounded form. In this case, each section is repeated AABBCCA. In section A the Leader, speaking in his own voice, states the charge against his family; in their response the Group intensifies the message by restating the Leader's line as a quotation (lines 1-2). In section B the abuse is shared—the Leader scoffs at the dead, the Group condemns the living (lines 3-4). The treatment of the theme reaches its personal and emotional climax in the C section in which everyone joins together to complain abjectly about mistreatment by their entire lineage (line 5).

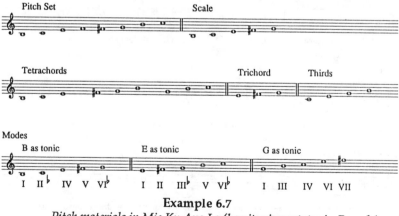

Example 6.7
Pitch materials in Mie Ku Ano Lo (hemitonic pentatonic, B mode).

When melody is taken into account the form is seen as A1A1 B1 B2 C1C2 A1. The two phrases in section A, each with two subphrases (1-2, 3-4), tonicize B and are repeated exactly (see Example 6.8). The first time through the text in section B, the Leader flirts with g as tonic, but then darts downward to B; the Group confirms the B tonicity (subphrases 5 and 6). In the repeat (B2) the Leader remains on g whereupon the Group ascends to b (subphrases 5' and 6'). In section C the powerful affect of line 5 is expressed

Example 6.8 *Melodic phrases in Mie Ku Ano Lo.*

in tune and rhythm. In the line's first performance, the tune briefly tonicizes c1, f♯, and e before settling on B (subphrase 7); in the repeat, however, the finalis is on e (subphrase 7'). Thus, section C is C1C2. The modulation to e in C2 functions as turnaround to the reprise of section A.

❹ *Melody, Mode, and Tonality*

I hear the tune in B, with E and G as complementary tonal centers: B-C-E-F♯-G (I-II♭-IV-V-VI♭), E-F♯-G-B-C (I-II-III♭-V-VI♭), and G-B-C-E-F♯ (I-III-IV-VI-VII). Two tonal axes, C-E-G and B-F♯, compete for tonic feel: although B and f occur as phrase finals, c, e, and serve as the main melody notes. We find three important types of melodic movement: 1) leap-step (M3- m2) movement within tetrachords (g-b-c1, b-g-f♯, e-c-B); 2) stepwise movement within the E-G trichord; 3) successive leaps in thirds (c-e, e-g).

The song opens in B (Section A, subphrases 1-4). As is true in the two anhemitonic songs, the Leader ascends into the uppermost range and then descends to the middle tetrachord. The Group continues in the mid-range and then drops to the low end of the range. In Section B1, the Leader hints at modulation to g but he and the Group fall back to B (subphrases 5-6). The Leader breaks through to g in section B2 (subphrase 5'), but the Group, rather than confirming the modulation, quickly moves upward to b. The B section contains new tonicity and ascending tessitura, again the same pattern found in *Gbe Yi Gbe Me Ku La* and *Xe Nǫ Ha Mee Me Nye*.

The similarity in overall organization between anhemitonic and hemitonic songs holds true in the C section, as well. Section C1 (subphrase 7) adheres to tonal/melodic patterns established in section A: ascent g-c1, descent b-f♯, undulation between c-e, and final on B. When the text is repeated, however, the melody modulates to e (subphrase 7'). Here, Mr. Agbeli purposely controls the distinction between f♯ and f♮: as a mid-phrase final (beat 2) he uses either the neutral or sharpened versions but as a pitch that leads to e as the new tonal center, he consistently intones f♮. On the other hand, during the three repetitions of the song on the audio cassette the intonation of F at other spots in the melody varies, seemingly at random. In both songs with extended rounded form (*Mie Ku Ano Lo* and *Xe Nǫ Ha Mee Me Nye*) the C section introduces new material that functions as a turnaround.

Once again we find that the melody usually mirrors the rise and fall of speech tones, but that contour is not determined by this linguistic factor.

L: Mĩe kúá-nò lô dèvíe nyē dé.
G: Fōnyēmēawó dê bé mìe kú à-nò lô dèvíe nyé dè {2x}
L: Mĩkpó kúkúawó nâm dá lò.
G: Gbágbèawó hâ gbònà.
L: Mĩkpó kúkúawó nâm dá lò.
G: Gbágbèawó hâ gbònà.
A: Fōnyēmēawó dê áwò nûm à- léa n̄kú nyè á- dzè tsieawō dzī

❺ *Rhythm*

This song contains several new rhythmic procedures—displacement, imitation, 2:3 with dotted- eighths, and the extended use of the upbeat 6-feel (see Example 6.9). Furthermore, it has what in my opinion is the most difficult rhythm in the entire corpus of twenty songs. Displacement occurs in sub-phrases 1 and 2: each consists of two short-long figures (ti ta), but in subphrase 1 the first tone is onbeat while in subphrase 2 it is a pickup. The fact that the whole phrase begins on beat one is highly unusual. The Group response presents a challenging rhythm: it begins on the third partial of beat two with a quarter-note triplet (phrased two three one) that culminates on beat four, then goes directly into dotted-eighth duplets in beats four and one, before "cooling off" with short-long figures. In other words, two types of cross rhythm happen in one phrase—1) 3:2, quarter:dotted-quarter (upbeat 6:4-beat) and, 2) 2:3, dotted-eighth:eighth.

Imitation between vocal rhythm and bell phrase is found in the Leader's part in the B section. I hear it as "ta ti ta ta ti ta," the same pattern of long and short tones used in bell strokes 6-4. The song rhythm, however, is set within beats three, four, and one—the bell within beats four, one, and two. This fleeting instance of canon is an example of the influence of the gakokoe part on song.

Appropriately enough, the "killer" rhythm is used for the climactic line of text in the C section, *Fonyemeawo de awo num alea be nku nye adze tsieawo dzi*. Like the Group part in section A, it is set to the upbeat 6-feel but in this case there are six tones which run from the third partial of beat two to the onbeat of beat two in the next bell cycle: 1) *Fonye-*, 2) *meawo,* 3) *de,* 4) *awo,* 5) *num/a-,* 6) *lea.* Four dotted-eighths follow: 1) -lea, 2) be, 3) nku, 4) nye. The syllable *-lea* can be called a **metric pivot** between the two rhythmic feels. Now the hard part: first, the syllable *nye* is held through the onbeat moment of beat four, and second, the final three syllables, *'dze tsieawo dzi*, are set to dotted-eighths that are displaced within beats four and one by one sixteenth. To put this analysis another way, within an overall metric setting of 12/8 the phrase switches from 6/4 (quarter in 12/8 = quarter in 6/4) to 2/4 (quarter in 2/4 = dotted-eighth in 12/8). As performed by Mr. Agbeli, the phrase's rhythm has an fluent, free feeling.

ⓖ *Conclusion*

Although this song has a distinct scale, its other structural features are in keeping with the patterns found in the first two songs. Once again, it is evident that composers not only use music to put across the meaning of a text, but musical design is valued in its own right.

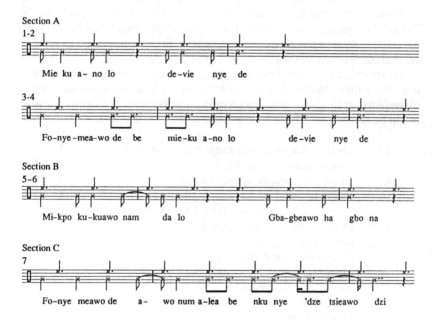

Example 6.9 *Rhythmic phrases in Mie Ku Ano Lo.*

AYODEDE SONGS (FREE RHYTHM)

The two *Ayodede* songs, *Agbemewo Me Si O* and *Me Li Eku Nava Tso* (Songs 11 and 12) are unique because they are sung freely in unmeasured rhythm. Judging from their texts, these songs date from the origin of the Kpegisu Drum in the Wodome-Akatsi area and are the oldest Kpegisu songs in this collection.

❶ *Text*

Agbemewo Me Si O refers to the beginning of Kpegisu in Wodome-Akatsi. As the song begins the Leader assumes the voice of *Sowu*, the hunter, and remembers when he was lost in the forest. Evidently, he was enchanted by forest spirits because the search party organized by his brother *Dogbeto* could not hear his cries for help. Speaking in an omniscient voice rather like a Greek chorus, the Group reflects, "The stirring stick dissolves in the drink." According to Mr. Agbeli, this could simply mean that hunters are most likely to face the forest danger, or it could be interpreted as a more general rumination on the consequences of destiny. After another reference to the episode of Sowu's disappearance, the Group comments, "If there is something for us to do in life, we do it." Not only does this specifically refer to the fact that Dogbeto used this adventure as the basis of a Drum, but also might be taken as another all-purpose comment on fate and duty.

L:	Me do leli agbemewo me si nam o he. {2x}	1
	Ye wo be ame ble na he.	2
G:	Ahablutsie ahame wo do na do.	3
	Dogbeto me si o.	4
	Sogbo be, "Ahablustie ahame wo do na do." {2x}	5
L:	Dogbeto do ame de Sowu de.	6
G:	Ne gbo ne gbo he.	7
	Ne agbenu ade li mia wo. {2x}	8
A:	Me do leli agbemewo me si nam o he. {2x}	9
	Ye wo be ame ble na he.	10
	Ahablutsie ahame wo do na do.	11
	Dogbeto me si o.	12
	Sogbo be, "Ahablustie ahame wo do na do."	13

L:	I shouted [but] the living did not hear me. {2x}
	And they said people get lost.
G:	The stirring stick dissolves in the drink.

Dogbeto did not hear it.
Sogbo said, "The stirring stick dissolves in the drink." {2x}
L: Dogbeto sent a person to Sowu.
G: He should come, he should come
If there is something for us to do in life, we do it. {2x}
A: I shouted [but] the living did not hear me. {2x}
And they said people get lost.
The stirring stick dissolves in the drink.
Dogbeto did not hear it.
Sogbo said, "The stirring stick dissolves in the drink."

Sung from Dogbeto's perspective, *Me Li Eku Nava Tso* is about the travails of a composer. As the Leader's lines reveal, the songmaker is resigned to a life of hardship and the inevitability of death. Why is he suffering? The Group response holds the clue—"A song, a song, do not rush me." In other words, he is fated to be a composer and must concentrate on singing at whatever the cost. Mr. Agbeli mentions a relevant Ewe adage, "The composer's farm is always weedy." Later in the poem we learn that even if the elders advise him to desist, a songsmith has no choice: "Can they come and tell me to rest?" But Dogbeto is not maudlin. He knows what he is doing and will accept the consequences. No one should pity him.

L:	Me li eku na va tso	1
	Dogbeto be, "Me li eku na va tsoe."	2
G:	Hae haee me ga yo nam o.	3
	Me li eku na va tsoe. {2x}	4
L:	Mega megawo na no anyi de he.	5
G:	Wo ava gbloe nam ma dzudzoa?. {2x}	6
A:	Me li eku na va tso	7
	Dogbeto be, "Me li eku na va tsoe."	8
	Hae haee me ga yo nam o.	9
	Me li eku na va tsoe.	10

L: I live for death to come and take me.
Dogbeto said, "I live for death to come and take me."
G: It is a song, it is a song, don't rush me.
I live for death to come and take me. {2x}
L: The elders should come and sit.
G: Can they come to tell me to rest? {2x}

> A: I live for death to come and take me.
>   Dogbetǫ said, "I live for death to come and take me."
>   It is a song, it is a song, don't rush me.
>   I live for death to come and take me.

❷ *Pitch Set and Scale*

Both songs use the hemitonic pentatonic scale (see Example 6.7, above). F♯ is rather consistently intoned. As is true in *Mie Ku Anǫ Lo*, melodic phrases occur within tetrachords (B-e, f♯-b, g-c1, b-e1) and the middle-range trichord (e-g). Leaps in thirds between C, E, G, and B are frequent.

❸ *Form*

Bothof these free rhythm songs have the rounded ABA form without a C section. Call/response relationships between Leader and Group are similar to those already discussed, although here the Group tends to specialize in wry philosophical commentary. Even when melody is factored into the analysis *Agbemewo Me Si O* retains a most basic A1A1 B1B1 A1 form; in *Me Li Eku Nava Tsǫ*, however, melodic development in the B section produces a A1A1 B1B2 A1 form.

❹ *Melody, Mode, and Tonality*

The tune of *Agbemewo Me Si O* can be divided into ten subphrases (see Example 6.10). The first line of the poem is sung twice: first, the melody rises from g to e1, falling back to b (subphrase 1); second, beginning without pause the repetition wavers between b-c1 before retracing the route g-c1 (subphrase 1'). Digressing for a moment to consider the impact of speech tone on melody, we see that the same text is set to two different melodies. This indicates that while melodic direction usually conforms to speech tone contour, language does not exert an all-controlling influence on music. Here is more evidence that the meaning of a song's text is clear even when its tune diverts from the sequence of speech tones. The Leader's part continues with a descent b-f♯ (subphrase 2). In the Group response (subphrases 3-7) each melodic unit ascends briefly before falling to progressively lower finals c1, f♯, e, f♯, and B. In section B the Leader's phrase centers on the e-g trichord, hovering at g before plunging downward m6 to B. The Group's phrase tonicizes e before moving to B (subphrases 9 and 10). To my ear, the repeated e-c-e leaps create the impression of resistance against the inexorable tonal gravity of B. Thus, although this song does not have a full-fledged turnaround, section B does contain increased tonal tension between the B-f♯ and e-g-c1 axes.

Many of the same melodic/tonal patterns occur in *Me Li Eku Nava Tsǫ* (see Example 6.11). In section A the Leader's phrase opens g-c1-b and closes on f♮ (sometimes f♯). The Group response is rather like the B section of *Agbemewo Me Si O*: g mediates between b and e, there is a m6 downward leap g-B, and e is tonicized before the finalis on B. Section B1 in both songs is al-

Example 6.10 *Melodic phrases in Agbemewo Me Si O.*

most identical but *Me Li Eku Nava Tso* has a B2 section in which the Leader truly tonicizes g. As was the case in *Mie Ku Ano Lo*, the Group then moves upward to b.

❺ *Rhythm*

These songs are unique in this collection because they are not timed to the bell phrase. There is a sense of pulsation and rhythmic drive within each phrase, but the duration of held tones and silences between phrases is unmeasured. The duration of tones within phrases is determined exclusively by speech rhythm. Perhaps it should be mentioned that my placement of phrases within an implicit 4-beat meter is based on Mr. Agbeli's performance of the songs while he clapped a steady 4-beat. According to him, songs of the Ayodede type can be transferred to dance time; I myself have heard songs from the *Atsiagbeko Drum* performed both in free and strict rhythm. Indeed, songs in bell time can be performed with the speech-like elasticity of the Ayodede.

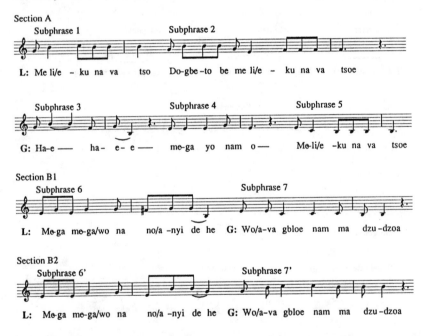

Example 6.11 *Melodic phrases in Me Li Eku Nava Tso.*

❻ *Conclusion*

Except for the unmeasured rhythm and long duration of phrase finals, these songs are very much like the three already discussed. Since three hemitonic pentatonic songs now have been discussed, perhaps it is time to offer some conclusions about melodic and tonal structure in this scale. The A sections are characterized by a bi-tonality between E and B. The pitch class E and its allies G and C are the axis of tonal resolution, but phrase finals are on B and the F pitch class (usually f♯). The B sections, on the other hand, contain stronger tonicizations of E, G, or C even to the extent of what I call modulation. Nevertheless, the B feeling is never far away, as indicated by the Group's immediate ascent to b if the Leader ends on g.

VUTSQTSQE SONGS (FAST PACE)

Vutsotsoe songs share the important features of musical style I have been discussing such as 1) the musical support for poetic meaning, 2) rounded form, 3) antecedent-consequent relationships within the call/response format, 4) hemi- and anhemitonic scales, 5) melodic sequence and tonicization within adjacent tetrachords, 6) bi-tonality and modulation, and 7) rhythmic counterpoint using 3:2, 2:3, syncopation, series of short-long pairs, and varying phrase lengths. Nevertheless, they do have characteristics which distinguish them from *Vu Blewu* and *Ayodede* songs besides the most obvious—their fast pace.

❶,❸ *Text and Form*

In fast-paced songs texts are often short, repetitive, and direct. For example, one idea may be restated over-and-over, giving the text a linear form A1 A2 A3 A4. The progression of tonal centers in these songs creates a rounded AABA melodic form, however.

> Kale nutsu agbadza dze wo he. Kale vava. {4x}
> Warrior, the war belt fits you. True warrior. (song 16)

> Kpogbale xoxoa le tsi gbe tsie fo. Nonoea vo wo nue {4x}
> The old leopard skin is left for the rain to beat. The spots are gone.
> (song 17)

Subjects may be mundane as in the song of complaint to the elders about liquor. As discussed below, when the melodic/tonal structure is taken into account the form of this song is A1A2 B1B2.

Miatǫ Bebeviawo, nua mele vivim o. {2x}   A1, A2
Nyabada 'nuglo nyae dzǫ, enuglo nyae dzǫ.   B1, B2

Fellow friends of Benin beer, the thing is not sweet.
Bad word, everyone is tired, everyone is tired. (song 18)

On the other hand, martial courage is a popular theme in these rhythmically rousing songs. It seems clear that this exciting, energetic portion of the
performance makes a good vehicle for the display of physical stamina and
grace under pressure. Although the war songs can be simple (see Song 16,
above), they also may have the full extended rounded form, A1A1 B1B2 C1
A2.

L: Da tum de ne sodgbe mi wǫ ge.   A1A1
G: Amewo da tum de ne sodegbe mi wo ge. {2x}
L: Amewo tsǫ tu.   B1
G: Tsǫ tu yi ava awǫ ge.
L: Amewo tsǫ yi.   B2
G: Tsǫ yi yi ava wǫ ge.
A: Ava wǫ nutsu ya me sia tu o de.   C1
     Be sodegbe mi wǫ ge.
A: Amewo da tum de ne sodegbe mi wo ge.   A2

L: [You] shot me with gun, on the fighting day we shall do it.
G: People shot me with gun, on the fighting day we shall do it. {2x}
L: People take guns.
G: Take guns and go to make war.
L: People take cutlasses.
G: Take cutlasses and go to make war.
A: A true warrior never fears gun.
     On the fighting day, we shall do it.
     People shot me with gun, on the fighting day we shall do it.

Some Fast Drumming songs may not be Kpegisu songs per se, but rather
are borrowed from other Drums such as *Afa*, a religious Drum (Songs 14 and
19). Mr. Agbeli reports that the songs most closely associated with Kpegisu
are sung in the *Ayodede* and *Vu Blewu*. Afa songs often contain references to
the castings used in the process of divining one's destiny. In the text below,
Yeku and *Abla* are names of casting configurations.

Bǫ legbe tǫ me dia nu do kpo o. Yeku dze Abla me.
A long-armed [generous] person does not search and fail. Yeku
gets into Abla.

As the above texts indicate, fast-paced songs often come right to the
point, aggressively. Yet even in these cases, indirection arises when a theme
is applied in a new context. A song ostensibly about hunting and war may
be intended as advice for right living. Mr. Agbeli says that the poem below
teaches that any serious work should be planned well and carried out with
seriousness.

Gidigidi me wua kpǫ o.
Kpǫ la wu gbe ada ḏo me.
Tua wui lo. Iye. Tua wui ḏe adzido gome.
'Meka be vie ma yǫ?

Rushing does not kill the leopard.
On the day of killing the leopard there should be seriousness.
The gun has killed it. Indeed! The gun has killed it under the
baobab tree.
Whose child shall I call? [to announce the news]

❷ *Pitch Set, Scale, and Mode*

The same scales are found in fast- and slow-paced songs. Pitch material in
the hemitonic pentatonic songs is identical but, as we shall see, the bi-tonal
tension occurs between C and B, not E and B as in the slower songs.
Likewise, the pitch sets and ranges for the anhemitonic songs are similar, although certain distinctive melodic/modal structures require different
added pitches. In this collection, anhemitonic melodies of the E mode type
are not found in fast songs. D mode melodies are favored, but their melodic
structure sometimes is quite unlike the slow melodies. One song (Song 19)
is unique; it is in what I will call the G mode—G-A-B-D-E (I-II-III-V-VI).

❹ *Melody and Tonality*

Most features of melody hold true in the fast-paced songs. In the hemitonic
songs—*Adzigo Adzigo, Bǫ Legbe Tǫ,* and *Soḏegbe Miwǫ Ge* (Songs 13, 14, 20)—
a difference occurs in the treatment of C and B in the upper b-e1 tetrachord

(see Example 6.12). We hear it immediately in section A. The Leader's first phrase tonicizes c1, not b as in the slow songs (subphrase 1). The rest of section A is "normal:" the Leader's finalis on f♯ (subphrase 2), followed by the Group's c-g movement and B finalis (subphrases 3 and 4). Section B in fast

Example 6.12
Melodic phrases in Sodegbe Miwo Ge
(hemitonic pentatonic; B mode; fast-pace).

songs is quite different from the slow ones: the Leader's phrase is set in the upper tetrachord and ends on c1 (subphrases 5 and 5'); the Group's phrases are set in the middle range and end on b (subphrases 6 and 6'). B and c1, in other words, are competing tonics.

In songs 13 and 20—two versions of the same song—this tug-of-war between Leader and Group is resolved in a C section sung by All. The long, undulating, rhythmically exciting phrase cadences to g (subphrase 7). The subsequent short phrase ending on f is the turnaround to the bi-tonal A section (subphrase 8). Although it is risky to make definite assertions about the ever-shifting intonation of the F pitch class, it seems to me that Mr. Agbeli purposely contrasts f♮ as upper neighbor of e and IV of c with f♯ as lower neighbor of g and V of B. For example, I hear f♮ in preparation for the cadence to B (subphrases 3-4); that is, c-e-f♮, g-e-c-B (I-III-IV, V-III-I- VII♭) with C as tonic.

Turning now to the anhemitonic songs (D mode; D-E-G-A-C; I-II-IV-V-VII♭) we find a new melodic structure: rapidly shifting modes and tonics. Let us begin with the three songs that have repetitive texts and linear form, *Kale Ṉutsu, Kpǫgbale XoXo*, and *Miatǫ Bebeviawo* (Songs 16, 17, and 18). Each song contains four antecedent-consequent phrases sung one after the other without repeat. The subphrases of Leader and Group systematically end on different degrees of the mode; in other words, the melodic structure of these songs is a progression through several tonicized pitches and then back to D. In most cases, the consequent phrase confirms the tonic of the antecedent phrase (Group confirming Leader), but at crucial locations tonal movement occurs in the second half of the phrase, thus propelling the song forward through its melodic/tonal progression.

The cadences which drive the progression of tonicized pitches rely on melodic sequence and imitation. For example, in *Kale Ṉutsu* (Song 16) the Leader's part in phrases 2 and 4 is an exact sequence in the middle and lower tetrachords (g-a-c1-g-c1-a-g and d-e-g-d-g-e-d). In *Kpǫgbale XoXo* (song 17) the pitch classes F and B♭ are added to increase the opportunities for exact imitation; for example, the commonly found ascending M2 cadence (c-d) is duplicated at g and c1.

Since the progression of tonicized pitches moves according to P4 affinities (D-G-C), the question may be asked: Does each song have only one tonic, or do tonics and modes change with each phrase? If we accept the first premise the songs are understood to move in a I-IV-VII♭-I progression; if we adopt the latter position the songs are understood to use three modes of the anhemitonic scale set on different scale degrees: 1) I-II-IV-V-VII♭ on D, G, and C; 2) I-II-III-V- VI on C and F; and 3) I-II-IV-V-VI on G. Either interpretation might suit Ewe musical thought.

There is one more song to discuss: *Gidigidi Me Wua Kpǫ O* (Song 15). In contrast to the fast anhemitonic songs with linear form, its poetic and

Example 6.13
*Melodic phrases in Gidigidi Me Wua Kpo O
(anhemitonic pentatonic; G mode; fast pace).*

melodic form resembles the slow-paced songs--A1A1 B1B1 A2. Like other fast-paced songs its melody is built on clear shifts between tonal centers; in this case the primary mode is I-II-III-V-VI (G-A-B-D-E) and the contrasting tonal centers are D (V of G) and A (V of D). Not only is the mode different, but the layout of the melody within the pitch set is unusual. The finalis is set in the middle of the mode: D-E-G-A-B (V-VI-I-II-III).

❺ *Rhythm*

As we have seen, fast-paced songs use two types of poetic/musical form: 1) a relatively sparse text set within four melodic phrases in a linear form, and 2) a more wordy text set within a rounded form. In the first type each line of text has its own rhythm. It seems to me that this repetitive rhythmic quality makes the tonal shifts more prominent: you hear the song as one rhythmic/melodic shape being moved around within the scale. Although a rhythm may be repeated exactly, Ewe composers use subtle rhythmic

Example 6.14
Rhythmic phrases in Kale Nutsu (anhemitonic pentatonic; D mode; fast pace).

change to good advantage. Consider the Leader's rhythm in *Kale Nutsu* (see Example 6.14). In phrases 1, 2, and 4 it consists of three short-long pairs followed by two long tones. The final two tones are synchronized with the gakokoe and the upbeat 6-feel. In phrase 3, however, the final syllable "he" (it is not a true word but rather a sound of emphasis and intensification) is omitted from the text so that the melody ends squarely on the beat four, "*dzewo*" ("fits you"). Wonderfully, this is the tune's exact moment of turnaround, that is, when the melody arrives on its most unresolved pitch (C as VII♭ of D). Thus, this seemingly insignificant rhythmic change is vital to the song's effectiveness.

The rhythmic structure of songs with the second type of poetic/melodic form resembles the slow- paced songs. As ever in Ewe music, counterpoint with the bell is the single most important rhythmic quality. The gakokoe phrase serves as inspiration for many vocal rhythms and imitation/displacement between vocal and bell phrases happens in virtually every song. Other rhythmic devices abound. Many vocal rhythms accentuate the upbeat 6-feel, especially within beat four, as we have just seen. Explicit 3:2 (onbeat 6:4-beat) usually happens within beats one and two in synchrony with the three-and-two handclap phrase (see *Sodegbe Miwo* Ge, Song 20). The implicit or horizontal form of 3:2 (ti ti ta ta) happens frequently and, together with the short- long pairs (ti ta, 3-1 and 1-2), is an important building block of rhythm. "Swing" eighths (see Chapter 4) are very typical; in fact, eighth-quarter figures habitually are "evened out" in performance (see especially *Gidigidi Me Wua Kpo O*, Song 15). On the other hand, true duplets (dotted-eighths) are rare and are saved for important words in the poem (see section C of *Adzigo Adzigo*, Song 13).

❻ *Conclusion*

Each song is a balanced rhythmic composition. In A sections the phrases are longer, the Group echoing the Leader's rhythm. In B sections the shorter phrases usually borrow an important rhythmic idea from section A and cycle it at a quicker rate. Section C phrases have their own new rhythmic design. After the developments in sections B and C the reprise of A feels like an old friend.

✳   ✳   ✳

SUMMARY

Although each song is unique, the ones discussed above exemplify characteristic features of others in the collection. A summary is appropriate (see Chart 3.1 for a summary of each song's form, scale and tonality).

General Description

Songs from each of the three sections in a performance have distinctive qualities. The slow-paced *Vu Blewu* songs set a standard for what we might call the "typical" Kpegisu melody: a tune develops within a rounded form using an ordered progression of musical attributes including call/response, tonic pitch, melodic contour, tessitura, phrase length, and rhythmic shape. While very similar in most respects, songs from the *Ayodede* section are unmetered and sung at a freely-pulsed, slow pace. Some fast-paced songs also share this "classic" style, but other *Vutsotsoe* songs have a special format: linear form, rhythmic repetition, and rapidly changing tonicity.

The typical song form is A1A1 B1 B2 A1. Leader and Group have relatively long phrases in section A. The Leader's phrase begins in the upper range and works its way downward to a finalis in the middle range; the Group phrase undulates within the middle and low ranges, ending on the lowest pitch in the pitch set. The melody is bi-tonal: two pitches compete for tonic feel. The A section is repeated exactly. In section B1 the phrase lengths are shorter and the rhythm is excerpted from a longer A section phrase. The Leader's phrase is set within the low-to-mid range and the Group phrase confirms its tonal center. The rhythm is identical in section B2 but the tessitura rises and the tonic shifts, a modulation that serves as a turnaround that drives the melody ahead into the reprise. Finally, Leader and Group join and sing the opening call-and-response together.

Tonality

Songs may be categorized on the basis of their tonality. Two pentatonic scales are used: hemi- and anhemitonic. All the songs with minor seconds (hemitonic) use the same pitch set and mode (B mode) but melodic structure differs between slow- and fast-paced tunes. Among slow-paced anhemitonic pentatonic songs we find two significant modal/melodic types (E and D modes); among the fast-paced songs there is another type of D mode melody, and a new anhemitonic pentatonic category (G mode). Thus, these Kpegisu songs may be classified within five tonal/melodic/-modal types (see Example 6.15): 1) B mode; 2) E mode; 3) D mode, slow-paced type; 4) D mode, fast-paced type; 5) G mode.

Pentatonic Modal Structure and Melodic Sequence

Even though many songs use more than five pitch classes, all melodic structure is pentatonic. To cite two "pentatonicisms": M3 or m3 trichords are the frame for stepwise motion, and step- leap or leap-step cells are common building blocks of melody. But such observations hold true for pentatonic

Example 6.15 *Summary of modes.*

songs from all over the world. More penetrating insight into the unique qualities of these songs is gained by focusing on the melodic processes of sequence and tonicization. We find that their pentatonic modes encourage melodic imitation within adjacent or overlapping tetra- and pentachords. Significantly, what can be termed **quartal sequence** is a widespread melodic structure; that is, a melodic cell spanning a P4 recurs at different range levels within the pitch set.

In the hemitonic pentatonic B mode, the sequenced melodic unit is a three-note cell with two intervals, m2-M3 (see Example 6.16). This unit recurs exactly within the low, mid, and high ranges (B-c-e, f♯-g-b, b-c1-e1). On the other hand, this same type of melodic cell is found in mirror image (m2-M3 and M3-m2) within the tetrachords c1-b-g and e-c-B. These melodic sequences contribute to the modal structure of the pitch set: a B-b octave frame is marked off by disjunct tetrachords (B-c-e and f♯-g-b), but a m9 frame, B-c1, is established by three consecutive conjunct units, tetrachord-trichord-tetrachord (B-c-e, e-f-g, g-b-c1). Thus, melodic sequence plays a vital role in establishing the bi-tonicity between B and C so characteristic of melodies in this tonality. Sequence can help explain other pitch material, as well; for example, replication of the intervals in descending cadences to f♯ and B (m2-M3-m2, c1-b-g-f♯, f♮-e-c-B) provides a rationale for the presence of both f♯ and f♮ in one song.

The fundamental unit of quartal sequence in the two most prominent anhemitonic pentatonic modes also is a three-note cell with two intervals, in this case, m3 and M2 (see Example 6.17). The cell is treated differently in each mode. As we have seen, tunes in the E and D modes all follow a three-fold path of melodic progression (from bi-tonicity to modulation to bi-tonicity) between tonicized pitches in conjunct tetrachords (I-IV-VII♭). But the two modes differ in their tonal centers—E-A-D versus D-G-C—and, consequently, the order of M2 and m3 intervals within their cadential

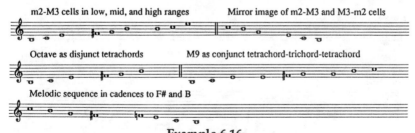

m2-M3 cells in low, mid, and high ranges   Mirror image of m2-M3 and M3-m2 cells

Octave as disjunct tetrachords   M9 as conjunct tetrachord-trichord-tetrachord

Melodic sequence in cadences to F# and B

Example 6.16
Melodic sequence in hemitonic pentatonic tonality.

phrases is inverted—E mode (m3-M2, e-g-a, a-c1-d1) versus D mode (M2-m3, d-e- g, g-a-c1). Certainly, the E mode tunes are distinguished by the m3 leap to and from tonal centers.

Other distinguishing features of modal structure are revealed through this type of analysis. The D mode, containing mirror images of the three-note cell within disjunct tetrachords (d-e-g, a-c1- d1), has a balanced structure within the octave; the E mode, with no 5th degree, is unbalanced within its octave frame. On the other hand, the P4 cell repeats in the high range level of the E mode (d1-e1-g1), making quartal sequence possible in three successive conjunct tetrachords. In the D mode sequence in conjunct tetrachords cannot continue into the high range because of the c1-d1-e1 trichord; the c-d-e trichord blocks a lower extension of quartal sequence in the E mode. These differences should not be exaggerated, however. The M2-m3 cell is a basic building block of melody in both modes and although the two modes may differ in the order of intervals within melodic phrases, their overall melodic effect is similar: movement in steps and leaps towards the tonal centers of adjacent tetra-and pentachords. Within the tune as a whole we hear a progression of tonicized pitches linked to each other by P4 affinity; within each melodic phrase we hear a characteristic set of intervals. As long as these tonal/melodic relationships are maintained, new pitches may be introduced either through melodic or harmonic process. This is seen clearly in the fast-paced D mode songs.

Given the Ewe predilection for quartal sequence and melodic imitation, we can understand why the I-II-III-V-VI or I-II-IV-V-VI modes of the pentatonic are rarely encountered. In the favored modes (I-II-IV-V-VII♭ and I-III♭-IV-VI♭-VII♭) the sequenced M2-m3 units recur throughout the pitch set (d-e-g, e-g-a, g-a-c1, a-c1-d1, d1-e1-g1) and equivalent melodies may occur within an intersecting network of tetrachords. For me, one of the most fascinating results of the "quartal" nature of these songs is that tonicized

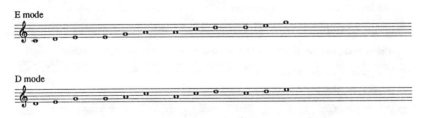

Example 6.17
Melodic sequence in anhemitonic pentatonic tonality.

pitches in the network of 4ths (I-IV-VII, II-V-VIII) are heard as melodic equivalents. In other words, pitches separated by intervals of a m7 or M2 (I-VII♭) can feel more in unison than an octave!

Rhythm

A song's rhythmic design is experienced linearly and vertically, that is, in terms of its internal shape and its relationship with the gakokoe phrase and the metric matrix. Except for one class of fast-paced songs, each song contains several distinct rhythmic phrases. Rhythms are made primarily with short and long tones (eighths and quarters); silence and an occasional held tone also come into play; combinations of sixteenths and dotted-eighths are rare indeed. Some rhythms may coincide with tones in the bell part, others create contrasting polyrhythm. Unisons are most common with bell strokes 4-7, the ones which match the upbeat 6-feel. Imitation and displacement of rhythmic motives borrowed from the gakokoe part are frequently used devices. Offbeat accentuation, especially on the third partial within dotted-quarter beats is accomplished by clever handling of speech sounds: a syllable with a prominent attack falls on the pickup, a syllable with a soft attack falls on the subsequent onbeat.[14]

Syllables of text often are sung as a series of short tones whose rhythm is open to interpretation by both performer and listener. Song rhythms may be understood to accentuate an implicit metric feel: two-note elements (ti ta) frequently accent the 4-feel; three- or four-note elements (ti ti ta ta) often accent the horizontal 3:2 cross rhythm between upbeat 6-feel and 4-feel beats, especially within 4-feel beats three and four. More than its onbeat twin, the upbeat 6-feel is highlighted in song rhythms. Cross rhythm primarily is 3:2 between quarters and dotted-quarters; 2:3 between dotted-eighths and eighths occurs sparingly, most notably in climactic lines of song text. Short-long pairs begun on the beat (1 2-3) usually are performed as "swing eighths."

Although songs may start at any moment within the gakokoe phrase, rhythms tend to move towards cadence on stroke 1, beat one. Even when phrases do not culminate on beat one, they derive important rhythmic flavor from that strongest of musical moments, as in phrases which end on bell stroke 7 (the twelfth eighth note in the measure). Phrase lengths are not constant. Indeed, the pleasing combination of different durations seems to be a crucial aspect of the art of song-making. Complete phrases frequently stretch over two bell cycles, but shorter phrases are more common. The duration of phrases is affected by song form—long phrases in A and C sections, short ones in B sections. Rhythms in B sections tend to be percussive, stark, and metrically oriented; rhythms in A and C sections are more flowing, ornate, and musically self- sufficient.

Text

Despite all the attention devoted above to musical qualities, it is vital to reiterate the analytical goal stated at the outset of this chapter: to show how a performer's experience of meaning derives from the synthesis of language and music. Although non-Ewe speakers may be tempted to hear the songs as "absolute" music, we will not grasp even the significance of musical structure through an exclusively formalist analysis. Decisions about form, melody, and rhythm are made with poetic themes in mind.

Music helps present poetic meaning. Repetition permits the contemplation of symbolism while modulation and melodic sequence reiterate with emphasis. Key words are placed on metric accents and/or given prominence in the rhythmic composition. The sections of musical form (A, B, and C) offer different imagery, related topics, changes in point-of-view. The shorter B section usually focuses attention on a vivid detail or vital action. In songs with a C section, the "punch line" of the text coincides with the climax of the tune. More simply, the sheer beauty of the music puts singers in the mood to receive the emotion of the poem. My point is this: the music of these songs is linked to the life experience of the singers.

Kpegisu songs are tuneful poems about profound subjects. Themes may be raised directly, but more typically they are invoked allusively through techniques of allegory, metaphor, change of voice, discontinuity, and so forth. Befitting Kpegisu's martial history, several songs retell old war stories, celebrate courage, and ridicule cowardice. The value of unity and generosity is praised; cooperative membership in funeral benevolent societies like the one to which the singers themselves belong is extolled. Songs teach values. Interestingly, in several songs the role of singer/composer is ruefully bemoaned as a source of poverty and stands as a symbol of bittersweet destiny.

Songs engage each singer with vital issues in an Ewe person's life: suffering, destiny, poverty, death, family, and self esteem. They are valued, it seems to me, because their meanings are relevant, insightful, witty, and impassioned. An exchange of ideas, emotion, and personality is at work: composers share their responses to existential problems with singers who are moved to heartfelt affect by the beautiful, communal expression of common sentiment.

Conclusion

To inject an Ewe perspective on the connection of music and culture, I conclude with a   quote from Mr. Agbeli. It was in the summer of 1990 on a day he and I had spent notating the speech tones and correcting the word-for-word translations of this song corpus. That evening he taught one of the songs to members of the Agbekor Society and as we left rehearsal I asked technical questions about speech tone, melodic contour, and an Ewe-speaker's experience of meaning: Is the meaning of text intensified when the tune goes a different direction than the speech tones? Does this musical contradiction of language attract attention? Does it make a person give special consideration to the meaning of words whose speech tones have been altered for specifically musical reasons? Do composers purposely craft tune and text with this feature in mind? "No," came his answer:

> *"Those questions do not go to the heart of how our composers create their songs. Rather, they think to themselves, 'How can I make this song in such a way that when people sing it, the emotion that I put into it, the things that are on my mind as I create it, will go into them deeply, strongly.' If it is a good song, the singers will be full of the feelings which inspired the composer. Music and text should suit each other. Singers should feel the meaning go into their hearts and they should make a personal connection between the composer's problems or insights and their own lives."*

His remark has guided my approach: text and tune work in tandem to communicate facts, ideas, and feelings.

✳   ✳   ✳

Notes

Preface
1. For insight into the socio-cultural context of Ewe music, I especially recommend the comparison of *Hausa* and *Igbo* music cultures in Ames; conclusions about the Igbo largely hold true for the Ewe.

Chapter One
1. Regrettably, there is no easily available study of Ewe history, society, and culture. Very helpful but obscure works on the Ewe people are those by Chapman, Manoukian, and Nukunya.
2. There is ample literature on these African people. The studies by Bascom (1969b), Busia, Fage, and Mercier are good introductions. See Herskovits for a longer classic study on Dahomey.
3. Mbiti provides a good introduction to African religions. See Fiawo and Riviere for detailed studies of Ewe religion.
4. See Little for a general consideration of voluntary associations in West Africa.
5. There is no exact correlate in English for the Ewe term "*vu*." Although Nketia (1963) uses the term "musical type," I follow my former student, Michael Frishkopf, in adopting the term "Drum."
6. Good summaries of the function of music (and dance) in human society are found in Merriam, A. Seeger, and Spencer.
7. Information on the *Agbadza, Kinka,* and *Brekete* Drums may be found in Jones (1959), Frishkopf, and Hill, respectively.
8. Ladzekpo, an Ewe musician himself, provides an excellent account of dance club performances.
9. See Jones (1959) and Locke (1987) for photographs and drawings of the musical instruments and more detailed discussion of playing technique.
10. Bascom (1969a) provides a wealth of information on this subject; also see Fiagbedzi (1979).
11. The late Hewitt Pantaleoni's doctoral dissertation is an excellent resource of information on *Atsia*. The Ewe version of *Kete* is quite different from the Akan Drum of the same name.
12. For an account of dance in Ghana see Blum.
13. For a very interesting account of the musical culture of *Adzogbo* see Conant.
14. By no means an expert on film-making, I gained important insight into the process by reading Heider. I am grateful to Barry Dornfeld for bringing this book to my attention.
15. Boateng provides a good overview of the geography of Ghana.
16. Diallo tells a sympathetic story of African spirituality from a modern, yet traditionalist African perspective.
17. Turnbull's classic popular ethnography of the Bambuti conveys the point about the value of participation in compelling fashion.
18. Nketia (1963b) introduces and develops the distinction between speech and dance modes of drumming.
19. I was sensitized to the martial significance of linearity in ground plans and movement style by reading Hanna.
20. The idea of sound as a simulacrum for existence is developed by the Sufi mystic Inayat Kahn.
21. Thompson (1973) develops the importance of the value of "coolness" in African aesthetics and philosophy.

Chapter Two

1. By no means am I the first to adopt this sequence of presentation; for example, see Qureshi.
2. Important issues in the notation of African music can be gleaned from Arom, Koetting, Kubik (1989), and Serwadda and Pantaleoni.
3. For a sampling of the discussion of transcription in the discipline of ethnomusicology see Jairazbhoy (1977), List, and C. Seeger.
4. My approach to the notation of rhythm has been strongly influenced by the writing of Creston.
5. I have not always adopted the convention of beaming to the beat. In *Drum Gahu* (Locke, 1987) I use beams to display the coherence of phrases.

Chapter Three

1. The Ghanaian scholar Kofi Agawu has emphasized the primacy of song in the African perspective on music (Agawu 1987).
2. *Se* as the personification of destiny is discussed at length in Koussou. I am grateful to my former student, Faith Conant, for bringing this work to my attention.
3. The metaphorical expression of the "us versus them" theme is prevalent in the War Drum *Atsiagbekɔ* (see Locke 1978). Vivid descriptions of inter-ethnic warfare in Ghana are found in Reindorf.

Chapter Four

1. The details of my career in African music are presented in Locke 1987 and 1990.
2. I first introduced this concept in Locke 1982.
3. Non-African musicians have been fascinated by this effect since the outset of modern scholarship in the field (see Hornbostel). The issue is thoroughly treated in Kubik 1962.
4. In this regard, I disagree with Jones who proposes a theory of multiple metric orientations in African rhythm (Jones 1954).
5. Good discussions of the rhythmic qualities denoted by the term "swing" are found in Gridley and Schuller.
6. See Cooper and Meyer for a thorough discussion of poetic "meters" in Western music.

Chapter Five

1. The topic of surrogate languages receives detailed treatment in Nketia 1971.
2. Berliner mentions a very similar phenomenon among *mbira* players of Zimbabwe. I suspect this is a characteristic of improvised music in many cultural traditions.
3. I first encountered the seed metaphor in Jones 1959.
4. Many authors comment on the connection between aesthetics and ethics in music (for example, see Chernoff).
5. A cautious attitude toward musical analysis is a tradition among ethnomusicologists; Herndon provides a good account of the issues.
6. The basis of improvisation in the bodily act of playing a musical instrument is well discussed by Sudnow and Kohut.

7. Maraire makes this point very persuasively for his Shona (Zimbabwe) tradition of *mbira* playing.

8. See Locke 1987 for a similar treatment of improvisation.

9. There is nothing particularly original in this model of improvisation; for example, Titon uses the concept of "preforms" in much the same way.

10. My ideas about what constitutes good analysis are influenced by the writings of Rahn. He mounts a healthy challenge to ethnomusicological shibboleths, as well.

11. In this, as in many other features of Ewe drumming, Jones blazed the trail (see Jones 1959).

12. That the "vibration" of which he speaks has a very strong tangible aspect was made clear when I toured the Media Lab at M.I.T. in 1989 with Mr. Agbeli, Midawo Gideon Alorwoyie, and Abubakari Lunna. The computer- and synthesizer-assisted "hyper instruments" left them decidedly nonplussed. As they put it, "We miss the physical vibrations of drum skins." I am grateful to Alice Lei for arranging this tour.

13. I first encountered the concept of "the deepened present" in the writings of Stone.

Chapter Six

1. I benefitted from discussion with members of my seminar in African music at Tufts University (Fall, 1991), especially James Kachulis. The analysis in this chapter is strongly influenced by Mr. Kachulis' keen ear and well-developed understanding of musical styles of European polyphony and American jazz.

2. Word-for-word translations, speech tone markings and rhythmic analysis for all twenty songs is available from the author who may be reached at the Music Department of Tufts University

3. Exploring links between the concepts "music" and "culture" is a defining feature of the discipline of ethnomusicology. Lomax proposes one of the most detailed theories for correlating features of cultural and musical style.

4. Agawu (1990), for one, does not refrain from musical analysis because of differences between insider and outsider perspectives; also see Pike, and A. Seeger on this issue.

5. Reference works I consulted included Appel and Arnold.

6. In adopting this approach I join prominent Ghanaian scholars of music such as Nketia (1963) and Agawu (1990).

7. The tonal systems of fixed-pitch instruments evidently require a different approach (see Kubik 1985).

8. My approach to modal analysis has been influenced by Adriaanz.

9. My analytical approach is influenced by Jairazbhoy's discussion of North Indian music (1971).

10. See Agawu (1990), Frishkopf, and Nketia (1963a) for discussions of Ewe "harmony."

11. See Dakubu.

12. Heider makes a good argument for the importance of presenting whole acts (and whole people) in cross-cultural reports.

13. See Agawu (1984 and 1988), Arom, Nketia (1963), and Schneider for analyses of the relationship between speech tone and melodic contour.

14. Kubik (1989) develops this point for Yoruba song.

Bibliography

Adriaanz, Willem. 1973. *The Kumiuta and Danmono Traditions of Japanese Koto Music*. Los Angeles: Institute of Ethnomusicology, University of California.

Agawu, V. Kofi. 1984. "The Impact of Language on Musical Composition in Ghana: An Introduction to the Musical Style of Ephram Amu," *Ethnomusicology*, 28/1:37-73.

_____. 1987. "The Rhythmic Structure of West African Music," *Journal of Musicology*, 5/3:400-418.

_____. 1988. "Tone and Tune: The Evidence for Northern Ewe Music," *Africa*, 58/2:127-146.

_____. 1990 "Variation Procedures in Northern Ewe Song,"*Ethnomusicology*, 221-243.

Ames, David. 1974. "Igbo and Hausa Musicians: A Comparative Examination," *Ethnomusicology*, 17/2:250-278.

Anyihodo, Kofi. 1983. Ph.D Dissertation. University of Texas at Austin.

Appel, Willi. 1966. *Harvard Dictionary of Music*. Cambridge: Harvard University Press.

Arom, Simha. 1991. *African Polyphony and Polyrhythm*. Cambridge: Cambridge University Press.

Arnold, Denis (ed.). 1983. *Oxford Companion to Music*. New York: Oxford University Press.

Bebey, Francis. 1975. *African Music: A People's Art*. Translated by Josephine Bennet. New York: Lawrence Hill.

Bascom, William. 1969a. *Ifa Divination*. Bloomington: Indiana University Press.

_____. 1969b. *The Yoruba of Southwestern Nigeria*. New York: Holt, Rinehart and Winston.

Berliner, Paul. 1978. *The Soul of Mbira*. Berkeley: University of California Press.

Blum, Odette. 1973. "Dance in Ghana," *Dance Perspectives*, 56.

Boateng, E.A. 1966. *The Geography of Ghana*. Cambridge: Cambridge University Press.

Busia, K.A. 1957. "The Ashanti," *African Worlds* (ed. Daryll Forde), pp.190-209. London: Oxford University Press.

Chernoff, John. 1979. *African Rhythm and African Sensibility*. Chicago: University of Chicago Press.

Chapman, D.A. 1944. "The Human Geography of Eweland (Anlo District)," *Premiere Conference Internationale des Africanistes de L'Ouest*. Comples Redus, Tome I, pp.79-101.

Conant, Faith. 1988. *Adjogbo in Lome: Music and Musical Terminology of the Ge*. 2 vols. MA Thesis: Tufts University.

Cooper, Grosvenor and Leonard Meyer. 1960. *The Rhythmic Structure of Music*. Chicago: University of Chicago Press.

Creston, Paul. 1964. *Principles of Rhythm*. New York: Franco Columbo, Inc.

Kropp Dakubu, Mary Esther (ed.). 1988. *The Languages of Ghana*. London: Kegan and Paul International for the International African Institute.

Diallo, Yaya and Mitchell Hall. 1989. *The Healing Drum*. Rochester, Vermont: Destiny Books.

Fage, J.D. 1959. *Ghana: A Historical Interpretation*. Madison: University of Wisconsin Press.

Fiagbedzi, Nissio. 1979. *Religious Music Traditions of Africa*. Accra: University of Ghana Press.

_____. 1977. *The Music of the Anlo*. Ph.D. Dissertation. University of California, Los Angeles.

Fiawo, D.K. 1959. *The Influence of Contemporary Social Changes on the Magico-Religious Concepts and Organization of the Southern Ewe-speaking People of Ghana*. Ph.D. Dissertation. University of Edinburgh.

Frishkopf, Michael. 1989. *The Character of Ewe Performance*. MA Thesis. Tufts University.

Greenburg, Joseph. 1966. *The Languages of Africa*. Bloomington: Research Center for the Language Sciences, Indiana University.

Gridley, Mark. 1978. *Jazz Styles*. Englewood Cliffs, NJ: Prentice-Hall, Inc.

Herskovits, Melville, J. 1967. *Dahomey: An Ancient West African Kingdom*. 2 vols. Evanston: Northwestern University Press.

Hanna, Judith. 1979. *To Dance Is Human*. Chicago: University of Chicago Press.

Heider, Karl. 1976. *Ethnographic Film*. Austin: University of Texas Press.

Herndon, Marcia. 1974. "Analysis: The Herding of Sacred Cows," *Ethnomusicology*, 18/2:219-262.

Hill, Richard. 1981. *Spirit Possession and the Music of the Blekete Cult of Southeastern Ghana*. MA Thesis. Legon, Ghana: Institute of African Studies, University of Ghana.

Hornbostel, Erich von. 1928. "African Negro Music," *Africa*, 1:30-62.

Jairazbhoy, Nazir. 1977. "The 'Objective' and 'Subjective' View in Music Transcription," *Ethnomusicology*, 21/2:263-273.

_____. 1971. *The Ragas of North Indian Music*. London: Faber and Faber.

Jones, A.M. 1954. "African Rhythm," *Africa*, 24/1:26-47.

_____. 1959. *Studies in African Music*. 2 vols. London: Oxford University Press.

Khan, Inayat. 1988. *Music*. Geneva, Switzerland: Sufi Publishing, Hunter House, Inc.

Koetting, James. 1970. "Analysis and Notation of West African Drum Ensemble Music," *Selected Reports*, 1/3:115-146.

Kohut, Daniel. 1985. *Musical Performance: Learning Theory and Pedagogy*. Englewood Cliffs, NJ: Prentice-Hall, Inc.

Koussou, Basile. 1983. *Se et Gbe: Dynamique de l'existence chez les Fon*. Paris: La Pensee Universelle.

Kubik, Gerhard. 1962. "The Phenomenon of Inherent Rhythms in East and Central African Instrumental Music," *African Music*, 3/1:33-42.

_____. 1985. "African Tone Systems—A Reassessment," *Yearbook for Traditional Music*, 17:31-63.

_____. 1989. "Anlo-Yoruba Chantefables: An Integrated Approach Towards West African Music and Oral Literature," *African Musicology: Current Trends* (gen. ed. Jacqueline Djedje), pp. 129-182. Los Angeles: African Studies Center & Africa Arts Magazine, University of California.

Ladzekpo, Kobla. 1971. "The Social Mechanics of Good Music: A Description of Dance Clubs among the Anlo-Ewe-Speaking People of Ghana." *African Music*, 5/1:6-22.

List, George. 1974. "The Reliability of Transcription," *Ethnomusicology*, 18/3:353-377.

Little, Kenneth. 1970. *West African Urbanization: A Study of Voluntary Associations in Social Change*. Cambridge: Cambridge University Press.

Locke, David. 1990. *Drum Damba*. Crown Point, IN: White Cliffs Media Company.

_____. 1987. *Drum Gahu*. Crown Point, IN: White Cliffs Media Company.

_____. 1982. "Principles of Off-beat Timing and Cross Rhythm in Southern Ewe Dance Drumming," *Ethnomusicology*, 26/2:217-246.

_____. 1978. *The Music of Atsiagbekor*. Ph.D. Dissertation. Wesleyan University.

Lomax, Alan. 1976. *Cantometrics: An Approach to the Anthropology of Music*. Berkeley: University of California, Extension Media Center.

Manoukian, Madeline. 1952. *The Ewe-Speaking People of Togo and the Gold Coast.* London: International African Institute.

Maraire, Dumisani. 1971. *The Mbira Music of Rhodesia.* Booklet and Record. Seattle: University of Washington Press.

Mbiti, J.S. 1970. *African Religions and Philosophy.* New York: Anchor.

Mercier, P. 1957. "The Fon of Dahomey," *African Worlds* (ed. Daryll Forde), pp. 210-234. London: Oxford University Press.

Merriam, Alan. 1964. *The Anthropology of Music.* Evanston: Northwestern University Press.

Nketia, J.H.K. 1963a. *African Music in Ghana.* Evanston: Northwestern University Press.

_____. 1963b. *Drumming in Akan Communities of Ghana.* Edinburgh: Thomas Nelson and Sons.

_____. 1971. "Surrogate Languages of Africa," *Current Trends in Linguistics: Linguistics in Sub-Saharan Africa* (ed. Thomas Sebeok), 7:699-732. The Hague: Mouton.

_____. 1974. *The Music of Africa.* New York: W.W. Norton & Company.

Nukunya, G.K. 1969. *Kinship and Marriage among the Anlo Ewe.* London: The Athlone Press.

Pantaleoni, Hewitt. 1972. *The Rhythm of Atsia Dance Drumming among the Anlo (Ewe) of Anyako.* Ph.D. Dissertation. Wesleyan University.

Pike, Kenneth. 1967. "Emic and Etic Standpoints for the Description of Behavior," *Language in Relation to a Unified Theory of the Structure of Human Behavior* [1954]. Glendale, CA: Summer Institute of Linguistics; The Hague: Mouton.

Qureshi, Regula. 1986. *Sufi Music of India and Pakistan.* New York: Cambridge University Press.

Rahn, Jay. 1983. *A Theory for All Music.* Toronto: University of Toronto Press.

Reindorf, Rev. Carl Christian. 1966. *The History of the Gold Coast and Asante.* Accra, Ghana: University Press.

Riviere, Claude. 1981. *Anthropologie Religieuse des Eve du Togo.* Lome: Nouvelles Editions Africaines.

Schuller, Gunther. 1968. *Early Jazz.* New York: Oxford University Press.

Schneider, Marius. 1961. "Tone and Tune in West African Music," *Ethnomusicology,* 5/3:204-215.

Seeger, Anthony. 1987. *Why Suya Sing.* New York: Cambridge University Press.

Seeger, Charles. 1958. "Prescriptive and Descriptive Music Writing," *Music Quarterly,* 44/2:184-195.

Serwadda, Moses and Hewitt Pantaleoni. 1968. "A Possible Notation for African Dance Drumming," African Music, 4/2:47-52.

Spencer, Paul (ed.). 1985. *Society and the Dance.* New York: Cambridge University Press.

Stone, Ruth. 1982. *Let the Inside Be Sweet.* Bloomington, IN: Indiana University Press.

Sudnow, David. 1978. *Ways of the Hand.* New York: Bantam Books.

Thompson, Robert, F. 1974. *African Art in Motion.* Los Angeles: University of California Press.

_____. 1973. "An Aesthetic of the Cool," *African Arts,* 7/1:40-43, 64-67, 89.

Titon, Jeff. 1978. "Everyday I Have the Blues: Improvisation and Daily Life." *Southern Folklore Quarterly,* 42.

Turnbull, Colin. 1961. *The Forest People.* New York: Simon & Schuster.

LIST OF MUSICAL EXAMPLES

LIST OF CHARTS

GUIDE TO TYPOGRAPHY AND PRONUNCIATION

e̱: sounds like e in men.

o̱: sounds like o in cost.

ḏ: an alveolar flap, like a Spanish r.

f̱: a voiceless bi-labial fricative, like blowing out a candle.

ṉ: a nasalized n, like ng in sing.

v̱: a voiced bi-labial fricative, like humming while blowing out a candle.

x̱: a velar fricative.

dz: one sound, like j in join, but with a little z sound added.

kp: one sound, like p in the back of the mouth.

gb: one sound, like b in the back of the mouth.

Also Available from White Cliffs Media!

Essential materials recommended by author David Locke:
1. *Kpegisu: Aural Examples. Audio cassette features performances of musical examples from the book, $12.95.*
2. *Kpegisu: Video Documentary Performance. VHS video filmed in Africa by master musician Godwin Agbeli, $79.95.*
3. *Kpegisu: Video Master Class. Godwin Agbeli performs sequences of Kpegisu, keyed to examples from the book., $59.95.*

The Performance in World Music Series—More great books, tapes!

The Drums of Vodou. Lois Wilcken featuring Frisner Augustin. Book, $19.95. Audio cassette featuring Frisner Augustin, $12.95.
The Music of Santería: Traditional Rhythms of the Batá Drums. John Amira and Steven Cornelius. Book, $19.95. Audio cassette, $12.95.
Drum Gahu: The Rhythms of West African Drumming. David Locke. Book, $15.95. Study tape, $12.95. Practice tape, $12.95. Field Tape, $12.95.
Drum Damba: Talking Drum Lessons. David Locke featuring Abubakari Lunna. Book, $17.95. Study cassette, $12.95. Studio Performance Video, $34.95. Stories and Drummed Language Video, $34.95.
Salsa!: The Rhythm of Latin Music. Charley Gerard with Marty Sheller. Book, $14.95. Audio cassette, $12.95.
Xylophone Music from Ghana. Trevor Wiggins and Joseph Kobom. Book, $12.95. Performance tape by Joseph Kobom, $12.95. Study tape, $12.95.
Synagogue Song in America. Joseph A. Levine. Book, $29.95. Three study tapes, $30.00.
The New Folk Music. Craig Harris. Profiles of leading contemporary folk and bluegrass singer-songwriters and instrumentalists. Book, $19.95.

Please order from your local book or record store!

Or order dire[Or order direct from White Cliffs Media, P.O. Box 433, Tempe, AZ]5, Tempe, AZ 85282. ℗ [85280-0433. Order line for credit cards orders: 1-800-359-3210 (orders]rs only). Add $2.50 plu[only). Add $2.50 plus .50 each item, maximum $5.00 for shipping/]ng. Visa, Mastercard, A[handling. Visa, Mastercard, American Express or check accepted. Prices] change over time.[subject to change over time.]

Distributed to the book trade by The Talman Company.